AN ENGLISH VIEW OF AMERICAN QUAKERISM

Memoirs of the

AMERICAN PHILOSOPHICAL SOCIETY

Held at Philadelphia

For Promoting Useful Knowledge

Volume 79

AN ENGLISH VIEW OF
AMERICAN QUAKERISM

The Journal of Walter Robson (1842-1929)
Written During the Fall of 1877, While Traveling among
American Friends

Edited by

EDWIN B. BRONNER

Haverford College Library

AMERICAN PHILOSOPHICAL SOCIETY
INDEPENDENCE SQUARE • PHILADELPHIA
1970

Copyright © 1970 by The American Philosophical Society

Library of Congress Catalog
Card Number 71-107345

TO

Emmalina Stanton Garretson
(1850—1931)

and

Blaine Garretson Bronner
(1894—1969)

Two Quaker ministers who would have enjoyed Robson's Diary

PREFACE

In the summer of 1964, while climbing Firbank Fell with a group retracing some of the early history of Quakerism, I fell into conversation with one of my fellow "pilgrims." Firbank Fell, near Sedbergh on the border between York-shire and Westmoreland, is rather wild sheepgrazing land today, just as it was more than three centuries ago when George Fox preached there to 1,000 local inhabitants. As we climbed the hill I talked about my recent research on the labors of a nineteenth-century English Quaker minister named Elizabeth Robson who spent four years traveling among Friends in America. When my companion told me that she knew about this minister, who was her great-great grandmother, I was thankful that my com-ments had been generally favorable, and was reminded that it is always dangerous to talk about one Quaker to another unless you know the family background.

A bit later my companion began to talk about her grand-father Walter Robson, and asked whether I knew of his visit to America in 1877. When I confessed ignorance, but expressed interest in learning more about him, she said that the family had his manuscript journal, and perhaps I would like to see it. When I read the "Journal of Walter Robson's Voyage to America, & Travels in the United States during the Autumn of 1877," I felt that it deserved a much wider audience. Based upon letters written to his wife Christina during the four months he was away from home, the journal, copied in longhand, presumably by Walter Robson, had been divided into five parts.

This is a literal transcription of the original except for a few minor changes. Slight changes of punctuation and alterations in abbreviations have been made. It seemed more logical to divide the journal into nine parts instead of five, and to begin a new paragraph for each daily entry. A few headings and personal greetings to the family have been omitted. Quaker terminology for days of the week and for the months has been retained. Thus, Sunday is First Day, and August is Eighth Month.

The original manuscript is in the possession of Hilda S. Ransome, of Birmingham, England, one of Walter Robson's sixteen grandchildren. Xerox copies of the original are in the Quaker Collection of the Haverford College Library, and The Library, Friends House, London.

A careful effort has been made to identify as many of the persons and places mentioned in the journal as possible. Biographical sketches of more than thirty of the prominent figures are provided at the beginning, and others are identified in footnotes. Much of this material has been taken from two "Dictionaries of Quaker Biography" presently in typescript. One has been compiled at The Library, Friends House, London, and is referred to as L-DQB. The other, prepared by William Bacon Evans (1875-1964) in the Quaker Collection of the Haverford College Library, is referred to as H-DQB. (See *Quaker History* **54** (1965): p. 45 for a fuller description.) Additional biographical information and background material have been obtained through the use of catalogs and files in these two libraries.

The work of editing this journal was supported by a grant from the American Philosophical Society, and by a grant Haverford College made from money provided by the Old Dominion Fund. Edward H. Milligan, Librarian in The Library at Friends House, London, read the entire manuscript and made many important suggestions. Henry J. Cadbury also read the manuscript and pointed out places where it could be improved. Phyllis Crockett Field prepared the original typescript from the journal. Staff members in the Friends House Library and in the Quaker Collection at Haverford were most helpful.

April, 1969   E.B.B.
Haverford, Pa.

CONTENTS

ILLUSTRATIONS

(The photograph for figure 1 was provided by the Robson family, and all other
illustrations are from the Quaker Collection, Haverford College Library.)

DRAMATIS PERSONAE

BALDERSTON, SAMUEL F. (1810–1895). Born in Baltimore, he married Martha Ann Griffith in 1835. A conservative Friend from the North Meeting in Philadelphia, he had been a minister since 1834. Some years had been spent in teaching, and he was known for his knowledge of the scriptures. He attended Baltimore Yearly Meeting unofficially. The *Friend* (Phila.) **68** (1895): p. 232.

BALKWILL, HELEN (later Harris) (1841–1914). Born in Plymouth, England, she went to America in 1877 for two years of service, accompanied by Susan Doyle of Ireland. She married Rendel Harris in 1880, and returned to America with him when he accepted academic posts at Johns Hopkins and Haverford. *Annual Monitor* (London) 1915: p. 106. Hereafter, *Ann. Mon.* L-DQB (see preface for explanation of H-DQB and L-DQB).

BEAN, JOEL and HANNAH (Shipley) (1825–1914, 1830–1909). Joel Bean was born in New Hampshire, and Hannah Shipley in Philadelphia. They were married in that city in 1859, and settled in West Branch, Iowa, where Joel Bean was living. They traveled together to the British Isles in 1872, and were well known to English Friends. After they moved to San Jose, California, in 1882, Iowa Yearly Meeting disowned them for unsound doctrine. Joel Bean was clerk of Iowa Yearly Meeting in 1877. *Ann. Mon.* 1911: p. 15; 1915: p. 12; *Quaker Biographies* 2nd ser., **3**: p. 211. Hereafter, *Qu. Biog.* H-DQB.

CHASE, PLINY EARLE (1820–1886). Born in Massachusetts and educated at Harvard, he married Elizabeth B. Oliver in 1843. A professor at Haverford, he was a linguist and scientist, and gave lectures on science and religion at Western Yearly Meeting. *Qu. Biog.*, 2nd ser., **5**: p. 199; *Dictionary American Biography*. Hereafter, *DAB*; H-DQB.

COFFIN, CHARLES F. and RHODA M. (JOHNSON) (1823–1916, 1826–1909). Charles Coffin was born in North Carolina, and Rhoda Johnson in Ohio; they married in 1847 and lived in Richmond, Indiana. Rhoda M. Coffin traveled in the ministry to Britain and the continent in 1871–1872. Charles F. Coffin was a banker and clerk of Indiana Yearly Meeting. *Charles F. Coffin, a Quaker Pioneer* (Richmond, Indiana, 1923); *Rhoda M. Coffin, Her Reminiscences . . .* (New York, 1910); *DAB;* H-DQB.

COMSTOCK, ELIZABETH (ROUS) (1815–1891). Born in Maidenhead, England, she taught at Ackworth School and elsewhere, married Leslie Wright in 1848 (d. 1851) and migrated to Canada in 1854. After marrying John T. Comstock of Michigan in 1858, she traveled almost continuously during the Civil War to visit prisoners, hospitals, and freedmen. She had returned to England for a visit in 1875, and participated in several American yearly meetings in 1877. *Life and Letters of Elizabeth Comstock* (London, 1895); *DAB;* H-DQB.

DOUGLAS, JOHN HENRY (1832–1919). Born in Maine, educated at Friends School, Providence, Rhode Island, he moved to Ohio in 1853. He married Miriam Carter in 1856, and was recorded as a minister in 1858. He traveled in the ministry in England and the continent in 1866–1867, and was a prominent evangelist who belonged to Indiana Yearly Meeting in 1877. *American Friend* **8** (1920): p. 17. (A new Series began in 1913.) H-DQB.

DOUGLAS, ROBERT WALTER (1834–1919). Brother of John Henry Douglas, he too was born in Maine and educated at the Friends School in Providence, Rhode Island. He married Margaret Ann Gifford, and lived in Ohio most of his adult life. He joined his brother in evangelistic work, and became a Friends pastor. He is said to have been the first Friends minister to perform a marriage ceremony, in contrast to the usual Quaker wedding practice. He made two journeys to Europe and one to Australasia during his ministry. *American Friend* **7** (1919): p. 239.

HANSON, JOHN F. (1841–1917). Born in Stavanger, Norway, his family joined the Norwegian migration to Iowa in 1856. He was recorded as a minister in 1868, and married Mary Hull. He first returned to Europe in 1873, and made five journeys to Norway in all. *Light and Shade from the Land of the Midnight Sun* (Oskaloosa, Iowa, 1903) includes some autobiographical material. *The Friend* (Phila.) **91** (1917): p. 177. H-DQB.

HOBBS, BARNABAS COFFIN (1815–1892). Born in Indiana, and married to Rebecca Tatum in 1843, he was an important educator. He served for a time as president of Earlham, and as Superintendent of Public Instruction in Indiana. A gifted minister, he accompanied Walter Robson back to England in the fall of 1877. The *Friend*, (London) **33** (1892): p. 217. H-DQB.

HUNT, DAVID (1806–1893). Born in Ohio, he was already a recorded minister when he moved to Iowa in 1857. The first clerk of Iowa Yearly Meeting when it was created in 1863, he traveled to Great Britain in 1866. *Friends Review* **46** (1893): p. 542. H-DQB.

JAY, ALLEN (1831–1910). Born in Ohio, he later moved to Indiana and married Martha Sleeper in 1854. His education included some time at Antioch College, and he taught school and farmed. His gift in the ministry was recognized in 1864. After the Civil War he moved to North Carolina to aid in the educational programs of that period. *Autobiography of Allen Jay* (Philadelphia, 1910), *DAB;* H-DQB.

JENKINS, GEORGE and SARAH (UPDEGRAFF) (d. 1879, 1818–1902). George Jenkins and Sarah Updegraff were both born in Ohio in the early days of that state and yearly meeting, and they were married in 1841. George Jenkins was clerk of Ohio Yearly Meeting and active in Indian affairs. His wife was an active minister and a sister of David B. Updegraff (*q.v.*), whom she accompanied to Kansas Yearly Meeting in 1877. *Friends Review* **32** (1879): p. 569; *American Friend* **9** (1902): p. 564.

KIMBER, ANTHONY (1824–1917). Born in Philadelphia, and married to Margaret Cooper Cope, he was a merchant in that city. He had traveled earlier with Isaac Robson, Walter Robson's uncle, and now volunteered to accompany the young English Friend to Ohio. *Biographical Catalog of the Matriculates of Haverford College* (Philadelphia, 1922), p. 17. Hereafter, *Biog. Cat. Haverford.*

KING, FRANCIS T. (1819–1891). Born in Baltimore and educated there and at Haverford College, he married Elizabeth Taber of New Bedford, Mass. After she died in 1856, he retired from business and devoted himself to the concerns of Friends. He was involved with care of freedmen after the Civil War, and was clerk of Baltimore Yearly Meeting for many years. The *Friend* (London) **32** (1892): p. 205. H-DQB.

KING, RUFUS P. (1843–1923). Born in North Carolina, he joined Friends in Indiana where he settled after serving in the Confederate Army in the Civil War. He was recorded as a minister, and was traveling in the ministry in Great Britain and on the continent from 1875 until late in 1877. He arrived in North Carolina in time for yearly meeting. *Qu. Biog.* 2nd ser. **2**: p. 175. H-DQB.

LADD, WILLIAM HENRY (1823–1890). Born in Ohio and educated at Haverford, in 1848 he married Caroline C. Coffin (sister of Charles F. Coffin, *q.v.*). An active Republican, he worked for the freedmen during and after the Civil War. He was a Friends minister, and lived in Brooklyn, N.Y., in 1877. *Biog. Cat. Haverford*, p. 38. H-DQB.

MALLISON, S. ELIZABETH (1834?–1881). There seems to be little specific knowledge about Elizabeth Mallison. She was apparently born in England, reared a Methodist, and Mallison is her married name. She was converted to Friends and recorded as a minister. She was active in the General Meetings, and an effective preacher. *Friends Review* **34** (1881): p. 810.

PUMPHREY, STANLEY and SARAH (GRUBB) (1837–1881, 1846–1932). He was English and educated at Ackworth. He retired from business in the early 1870's and spent full time in Gospel ministry. He was in America from 1875–1877, and was concerned with the Indian question in addition to visiting among Friends. He married his second wife, Sarah Grubb, in 1877 and took her to America for a second period of ministry. Sarah Pumphrey remained active in Quaker affairs in the years after her husband's death. *The Young Man of God, Memories of Stanley Pumphrey* (London, n.d.). L-DQB.

RHOADS, DR. JAMES (1828–1895). A Pennsylvanian, he did his medical study at the University of Pennsylvania. He married Margaret Wilson Ely in 1860, and a few years later began to give full time to Quaker concerns. He was president of the Indian Rights Association, editor of the *Friends Review* from 1876 to 1884, and first president of Bryn Mawr College. "Memoir of James E. Rhoads," *Proc. Amer. Philos. Soc.* **34** (1895). *DAB;* H-DQB.

ROBSON, WALTER (1842–1929). Born in England, he met and married his wife Christina Cox, in Australia in 1869, while accompanying Joseph J. Neave in travel in the ministry. A draper in Saffron Walden, he was recorded as a minister in 1871. A gifted evangelical preacher, he remained active in civic and Quaker affairs after his return from America. The *Friend* (London) **70** (1930): p. 35. H-DQB.

SATTERTHWAITE, SARAH (CARRICK) (1818–1913). An English Friend, and the widow of Michael Satterthwaite, she made several journeys to America, beginning in 1872. In 1882 she married James Clark, and they traveled together in the ministry. *Ann. Mon.*, 1914: p. 28. L-DQB.

SMITH, HANNAH (WHITALL) (1832–1911). A Philadelphia Friend, she married Robert Pearsall Smith in 1851. Both of them were active evangelists, and Hannah Whitall Smith was the author of several books including *The Christian's Secret of a Happy Life.* *A Family of Friends, the story of the Transatlantic Smiths* (London, 1960); *DAB;* H-DQB.

TALBOT, CAROLINE E. (LAWRENCE) (1826–1894). Born a Methodist, in 1844 she married the Quaker, Kinsey Talbot, and eventually joined Friends. After she was recorded as a minister in 1862, these Ohio Friends traveled together to England in 1875, where Caroline Talbot visited in the ministry. *Friends Review* **48** (1894): pp. 198–200. H-DQB.

THISTLETHWAITE, HANNAH (SATTERTHWAITE) (1815–1893). An English Friend, and the widow of William Thistlethwaite, she was a recorded minister on her first visit to America. She was a sister-in-law of Sarah Satterthwaite (*q.v.*) L-DQB.

THOMAS, DEBORAH C. (HINSDALE) (1817–1889). Born in a New York Quaker home where ministers such as Stephen Grellet and Joseph John Gurney were entertained, she was recorded as a minister when a young woman. In 1859 she married Dr. Richard Thomas of Baltimore, and although he died the following year, she remained in that city. She went to Britain in 1874 and again in 1883. *Ann. Mon.*, 1890: pp. 200–207. H-DQB.

UPDEGRAFF, DAVID BRAINARD (1830–1894). Born in Ohio and educated at Haverford, David Updegraff was a gifted minister and evangelist. His first wife, Rebecca B. Price died, and in 1866 he married Eliza J. C. Mitchell. He is said to have been the first Friend to use "altar calls" in Quaker Meetings, and later in his career he was one of the Ohio Friends to advocate the use of the ordinances. *David B. Updegraff and His Work* (Cincinnati, Ohio, 1895).

VALENTINE, JULIA (THOMAS) (1808–1892). Her parents were former Friends and slave owners when she was born, but returned to Quakerism and freed their slaves. She married Bond Valentine of western Pennsylvania, but after he died in 1862, she returned to Baltimore. An active minister, she traveled in the ministry among Friends on both sides of the Atlantic. She is a sister-in-law of Deborah C. Thomas (*q.v.*). *Friends Review* **45** (1892): p. 740.

INTRODUCTION

Walter Robson's visit to the United States came at a crucial time in the development of new patterns in the Religious Society of Friends, especially in the Middle West. The revival movement had swept over Ohio and Indiana as well as the groups further west, and the responses to this phenomena were being felt in 1877.

The leaders of the various Quaker groups he visited accepted him with open arms, for he was completely orthodox in his theology, and it was obvious that he had a loving feeling for, and a deep appreciation of, his fellow religionists in America. At the same time, Walter Robson maintained a degree of objectivity during these extensive visits, which enhances the value of his observations. Orthodox evangelical Christianity in London Yearly Meeting was quite different from what he saw in Ohio and elsewhere, and this provided the author of the journal with a perspective which was highly significant.

Walter Robson had boundless energy, which led him to do and see as much as possible during every waking hour. From the time he dashed into St. George's Hall in Liverpool, to listen to a court case, on his way from the railway station to the dock where he took a tug out to his ship, to the end of his 12,000 miles of travels four months later, he was eager to take advantage of every opportunity to learn something new, as long as it was edifying. Fortunately, his energy did not flag at the end of a long day, for he compiled full, illuminating letters to his family at home, which are the basis of this journal.

One assumes that he found time to record his impressions daily, for he included many precise references, such as snatches of conversation and religious messages, as well as

1

statistics and facts, which he would need to record immediately before they were forgotten. He mentioned scores of Friends by name, and usually spelled names and strange words accurately, although there were some errors resulting from the combination of American accents with his English one, especially in the south.

Walter Robson was thirty-five years old when he undertook this grueling visit among American Friends, younger than most of the leaders he associated with. His companion from Philadelphia to Ohio, Anthony Kimber, was eighteen years older, and the minister who returned with him to England at the end of the journey, Barnabas Hobbs, was twenty-seven years older. David Updegraff, one of the leading ministers of the period was twelve years older, and most of the women ministers were much his senior. On the other hand, his fellow Englishman, Stanley Pumphrey, was only five years older, and there were a few other ministers about his own age.

A decade earlier, in 1867, Walter Robson had accompanied Joseph James Neave in travel in the ministry to Australia, Tasmania, and New Zealand.[1] On that occasion he went as a companion, for he was not recorded as a minister by Thaxted Monthly Meeting, in Essex, until 1871.[2] It was before that same body, in March, 1877, that Walter Robson placed his concern, "which had rested on his mind for a year," to visit American yearly meetings.[3] The Yearly Meeting on Ministry and Oversight of London Yearly Meeting, the national body in England, gave its

---

[1] J. J. Neave (1836–1913), as he was usually called, traveled extensively among Friends during his life. He had made a most important, and highly dangerous visit to Friends in North Carolina, Virginia, and Tennessee just at the end of the American Civil War. See his: *Leaves from the Journal of Joseph James Neave* (London, 1910). H-DQB.

[2] The *Friend* (London) **11** (1871): p. 182.

[3] *British Friend* **35** (1877): p. 117. The announcement closed with this sentence, "Nothing but concurrence being expressed a certificate was agreed to be prepared for him."

approval in May, and thus he went with official sanction to the sister yearly meetings in the United States.[4]

Walter Robson was born at Saffron Walden, in Essex, a market town fifteen miles south of Cambridge, on March 30, 1842, the son of John Stephenson Robson and Rachel Green. He was the youngest of five children, and was educated in a school at Weston-Super-Mare, on the Bristol Channel, run by Till Adam Smith, formerly a master at Bootham. He then entered the family business, a firm started by his great-grandparents, Thomas and Susannah Day, in 1760, but called Robson, Green & Co. at that time. He remained active in the drapery business until he retired in 1913.

While in Australia, he met Christina Cox, daughter of George Cox, of Wollongong, near Sydney, and they were married out there in 1869. The couple returned to Saffron Walden, and had five children, two sons and three daughters, by 1877. A sixth child was born to them in 1880. Walter Robson was active in the borough of Saffron Walden and in the Society of Friends for the remainder of his long life. He served as borough treasurer for twenty-five years, and as a magistrate. He was clerk of both his monthly and quarterly meeting, and was on the committee for Saffron Walden Friends School for more than half a century. The couple celebrated the sixtieth anniversary of their wedding late in 1929, and Walter Robson died six weeks later, on December 14.[5]

He had continued his public ministry during this long and useful life, and The *Friend* said, "The death of Walter Robson would seem to signal the closing of an era in the

[4] *Extracts from the Minutes and Proceedings of the Yearly Meeting of Friends, Held in London,* 1877: p. 12. Hereafter, London Y.M. *Proceedings.*

[5] *Pease of Darlington,* compiled by Joseph Foster (privately printed, n.p., 1891), pp. 61, 62; The *Friend* (London) **70** (1930): pp. 35, 36.

Society of Friends, this passing of almost if not quite, the last of the great ministers of the nineteenth century."[6]

Walter Robson left Saffron Walden on August 7, 1877, accompanied by his father, and traveled to Huddersfield in order to talk with his uncle, Isaac Robson, who had made a similar journey to America in 1870.[7] He went on to Liverpool the next day, and sailed on the *Pennsylvania* that evening. During a fairly uneventful crossing, Robson conducted religious services one Sunday evening, and on another occasion delivered a lecture to the passengers on missionary work in the South Pacific area, a speech he was to give many times in the next four months. They landed in Philadelphia on Sunday, August 19.

After a brief stay with Dr. James Rhoads, editor of the *Friends Review,* the Gurneyite publication in Philadelphia, he traveled by train to Mount Pleasant, Ohio, for Ohio Yearly Meeting. Robson was greatly dismayed by the informality and religious enthusiasm of this, his first American yearly meeting. The shouting, singing, and the lack of the sober decorum he was accustomed to in London was most disconcerting. He wrote home asking his family to pray, "that I may overcome my too keen sense of the ludicrous."

When Ohio Yearly Meeting ended on August 30, Robson left for Cleveland for a brief visit with Friends, then to Chicago for a similar stay, and on to Oskaloosa, Iowa, where yearly meeting opened on September 4. During Iowa Yearly Meeting the Conservative Friends, largely from Bear Creek Quarterly Meeting, who objected to the direction the yearly meeting was taking, broke away and set up a separate body. Both Robson and Stanley Pumphrey joined Iowa Friends in serious efforts to heal

---

[6] *Ibid.*

[7] Isaac Robson (1800–1885) was recorded as a minister in 1844. In addition to his visit to America, he traveled to Italy to labor among protestants there, and to southern Russia to visit the Mennonites. L-DQB.

the breach, but to no avail. A similar situation developed in Western Yearly Meeting, at Plainfield, Indiana, the next sessions these two English ministers attended.

After the proceedings at Oskaloosa, several ministers including Robson took the train to Indianapolis, where they attended the funeral for Rufus King's mother, and then went on to Plainfield a few miles to the southwest. It was here that the visiting minister first experienced a western yearly meeting Sunday, when thousands of extra persons would pour into town for a day of picnicking, preaching, and conviviality. It was estimated that 12,000 went to Plainfield that day in carriages, wagons, and other conveyances. Railroads often ran special excursions for yearly meeting Sunday. Booths and stalls were set up along the streets to sell refreshments, "all teetotal," Robson assured his readers. He added, "many only come for the spree of the thing, but I trust some 'who come to scoff, remain to pray.'" A platform was set up outside the meetinghouse, where preachers addressed 5,000 persons, and others led the crowd in the singing of hymns.

Walter Robson had five days between the end of Western and the beginning of Indiana yearly meetings. He used that time to hold public meetings in various Quaker communities in Indiana, and also preached at a women's reformatory in Indianapolis. He felt uneasy about these meetings where he was expected to preach, and where Friends and other came to hear him, but afterwards always recorded his belief that God had led him in his words and actions. At the end of these sessions he had another period of several days in which he held more public meetings in Indiana and at Cincinnati.

Indiana Yearly Meeting, held at Richmond, followed the pattern of the previous three, and Robson entered wholeheartedly into it. On the Sunday night, after another big day with thousands of visitors, David Updegraff and

John Henry Douglas held a revival meeting at the meeting-house, what Robson called "an Altar of prayer." He continued, "Friends old & young—smart & very plain, kneeling in rows—sometimes quite still—often ejaculating short earnest prayer for a baptism of the Holy Ghost—some praising God with a loud voice that their prayers were answered . . . it was a scene never to be forgotten."

Once again accompanied by several other ministers, on October 9 Robson set off for Lawrence, where Kansas Yearly Meeting would soon convene. In addition to the Quakers in attendance, a number of Indians were present, for the territories where Friends worked with the aborigines were not far away. The evangelical preaching of Updegraff, Robson, and others aroused opposition from the minority in the yearly meeting which split off three years later. One old Friend arose while Robson was preaching to say, "Friends—I wish we might have a really solemn sermon in the life, instead of this light lifeless talk which only causes levity." Many others encouraged the English visitor to continue, and he did so despite the interruption. He had to leave the Kansas Friends before they concluded their sessions, in order to reach his next appointment, Baltimore Yearly Meeting.

Although Walter Robson tried to accept western Quakerism, and entered fully into all aspects of the work of the five yearly meetings he had visited, he did not refrain from making the following observation:

> It is a curious fact that the Alleghany Mountains seem to cut quakerism in two parts. *West,* they are all liberal in their actions as churches, *east* they are more like England—prudent, solemn & inclined to be conservative; no hymns sung; friends rise during prayer, periods of silence are observed, & altogether after the five Western Y.M.'s I have attended, the change to the proprieties of Baltimore is quite curious.

A number of Friends came down from Philadelphia to share in the sessions, even though the two bodies did not carry on official correspondence with one another. The Hicksite Friends of Baltimore attended some of the public meetings, and Robson felt he had a special message for such persons. When these meetings concluded, he left for Washington, Richmond, Virginia, and reached New Garden, North Carolina, on November 1.

Ministers had come from a number of yearly meetings to share in North Carolina Yearly Meeting, for many felt a concern to give support to this group of Friends who were still recovering from the Civil War and its aftermath. There were no hotels nearby, and not enough Friends' homes to entertain those attending yearly meeting. As a result, the New Garden Boarding School closed during the sessions and sent the students home, in order to provide accommodations. Space was at a premium, and it was not uncommon for guests to sleep three in a bed. Walter Robson had heard of this practice, and was greatly relieved to learn that he was to have a room to himself in a nearby Friend's home. Other Friends camped out around the meetinghouse, as they had done in Iowa, and the fires scattered through the woods, in front of tents or beside wagons, made an interesting sight, especially at night.

When North Carolina Yearly Meeting ended, Robson took the train and rode straight through to New York, where William Ladd met him and took him to his home in Brooklyn. After holding some public meetings in New York, he left by train for Niagara Falls. He "did" the Falls in one day, and took an overnight train for Philadelphia, not neglecting to record his personal reactions to this great natural wonder as the railroad transported him to his next appointments. In Philadelphia he spoke several times, and was invited to share the gallery in the North Meeting, at Sixth and Noble Streets, where the most conservative Friends of Philadelphia worshiped.

He returned home on the *Pennsylvania* which had brought him to America in August. One Sunday the sea was too rough for any religious service, but he preached on the following Sunday, and gave his South Seas lecture one evening. He reported that "Sankey's hymns are constantly being sung by some of us," even though the pianist, the wife of the Spanish Consul, was more familiar with opera than gospel hymns. On their last night, while crossing the Irish Sea, the ship struck and sank a large sailing vessel, the *Oasis,* but fortunately all on board were saved. When they landed at Liverpool on Tuesday morning, December 4, Robson and his companion Barnabas Hobbs, who was coming to England for an extended period of travel in the ministry, took the train for London.

After turning the American over to J. Bevan Braithwaite, Walter Robson took a cab for Liverpool Street Station, where his wife Christina was waiting for him, and they traveled home together. He concluded the journal with a paragraph praising God for watching over him during 12,000 miles of travel in four months, for enabling him to minister in a helpful way to the many persons he had touched, and for blessing "my own soul with a wondrous realization of the exceeding greatness of His power even to me, . . . His poor child."

Walter Robson was following an ancient tradition of Friends in undertaking this travel in the ministry. Ever since George Fox had begun to gather followers in the middle of the seventeenth century, there had been concerned persons who felt led to undertake religious visitation. The Quakers rejected professional training and learning as a qualification for such service. The important thing was that the person, man or woman, should be divinely blessed with a spiritual gift which enabled him to share religious truths with others, and to reveal God to them. Although Robson was a draper by trade, his "gift in the ministry" had been recognized in 1871, and it was not unexpected that he now had a concern to travel among Friends in America.

More than one hundred Friends traveled from Britain and Ireland to America before 1700 to minister among fellow Quakers and others. Seven of that group died in America, including those hanged on the Boston Common. In the first half of the eighteenth century, fifty-six ministers traveled in a westward direction across the Atlantic, and by that time, forty-four men and women went over from America to minister in the British Isles and Europe.[8]

In the last half of the eighteenth century, forty-seven went over to America, while sixty-three Americans crossed the Atlantic to travel in London Yearly Meeting, Dublin Yearly Meeting, and on the European continent. Nine of the Americans died, including John Woolman in England, Job Scott in Ireland, and John Pemberton at Bad Pyrmont in Germany.

Travel in the ministry continued in the nineteenth century. The Napoleonic wars at the beginning of the period severely curtailed this visitation, but it flourished during the remainder of the century. With the development of the trans-Atlantic steamer in the 1830's, the long voyage which had sometimes taken three months could then be made in a matter of days.

These men and women helped local meetings to gain new adherents through preaching in public meetings, and in personal visitation. They provided advice to Quaker groups which were troubled by matters of discipline. They served to keep the peace testimony strong, and helped to convince all Friends that they should oppose slavery. The traveling Friends reminded those they visited of other concerns such as the responsibility for Indians, for the mentally ill, or for those in prison. They preached the word of God and called Friends to be faithful to the Christ Within.

During the seventeenth and eighteenth centuries there

---

[8] These figures are based upon lists in The Library, Friends House, London, compiled under the title, "Quaker Trans-Atlantic Journeys."

was a single Religious Society of Friends, but beginning in 1827, there were separate branches of American Quakerism. The first schism, which began in Philadelphia in 1827, was believed to be entirely theological by the participants, but it is obvious today that there were important sociological aspects of the situation as well. One branch believed that the other denied the divinity of Christ, the doctrine of the atonement, and the divine inspiration of the scriptures. The other group protested that these accusations were untrue, and their *Books of Discipline* bear out their statement.[9] We know today that at least a part of the cause for the schism was a feeling of alienation of one group of Quakers from the other. The group called "Orthodox" was largely urban, rather more prosperous than the other group, and included a substantial majority of ministers and elders. The others, labeled the "Hicksites," were predominantly rural, less successful in business, and more of what might be called the rank and file of the Society, although there were many exceptions to these generalizations.[10]

[9] This brief description of the nineteenth century separations is based upon chapter one, "An Historical Summary," in *American Quakers Today* which I edited for the Friends World Committee for Consultation (Philadelphia, 1966).

[10] The "Hicksites" were named for Elias Hicks (1748–1830), a Long Island farmer who had traveled widely among Friends, and believed the so-called Orthodox were deviating from true Quaker principles. He had no desire to lead a separation, and was not in Philadelphia in 1827 when the split took place. In 1828 Orthodox-Hicksite schisms came in New York, Baltimore, Ohio, and Indiana yearly meetings. Only New England and North Carolina yearly meetings, plus the small group in Virginia which later merged with Baltimore, escaped this split.

In 1877 there were three distinct groups of Friends in the United States.

Orthodox		Hicksite	Wilburite
New England	Ohio	New York	New England
New York	Indiana	Philadelphia	Ohio
Philadelphia *	Western	Baltimore	
Baltimore	Iowa	Ohio	
North Carolina	Kansas	Indiana	
		Illinois	

* Philadelphia was not in official correspondence with the other American yearly meetings.

There were some 200 "Primitive Friends" in New York and Pennsylvania, who were somewhat similar to Wilburites. The two new yearly meetings formed

The Orthodox branch tended toward the evangelical movement of the period, which had ties with the Methodist movement, while some Hicksites were more sympathetic with the rationalism of the eighteenth century and the growth of Unitarianism in the nineteenth. In 1827, however, the two branches of Friends were closer to one another than they were to these external movements, although they were unable to recognize that fact.

London Yearly Meeting was also becoming more evangelical in outlook in these years, and many of the ministers who traveled from England to America were evangelical. Thus they were attracted to the Orthodox and were repelled by the Hicksites. Among those traveling ministers was Elizabeth Robson, the grandmother of Walter Robson, who is frequently mentioned in the journal.[11] She honestly believed that those with so-called Hicksite tendencies were highly dangerous to the Society, and often directed her preaching against them, just as her grandson did half a century later.

London Yearly Meeting decided that it could recognize but one branch of the Society of Friends in America, the so-called Orthodox yearly meetings, and that it would not communicate with the Hicksites. This meant that London did not exchange epistles, as the annual letters of fraternal greeting were called, nor would it encourage traveling ministers to have anything to do with Hicksites in America. Since Dublin Yearly Meeting made a similar decision, the Hicksites were cut off almost entirely from other groups of Friends. For the first few years after the separations, the Hicksites did not mind this ostracism, but before the American Civil War broke out some of their number were

in 1877 by "Conservatives," Iowa and Western, were also similar to the Wilburites.

[11] Elizabeth (Stephenson) Robson (1771–1843) was recorded as a minister in 1810, and made many religious journeys in the British Isles before she went to America in 1824 to travel and preach for four years. She returned to America for a shorter visit in 1838. L-DQB.

hoping to re-establish communication. Samuel M. Janney, the Virginia leader, and author of several books, was active in such efforts.[12] Hicksites attended public meetings arranged by the Orthodox, especially when overseas visitors were present, and this is why Hicksites came to hear Walter Robson on several occasions. In 1857 London Yearly Meeting did send a message to all "those who bear the name of Friends," but this was regarded as an exception, and was not expected to lead toward the renewal of official correspondence.

In the meantime, within the Orthodox branch a new division began to emerge. One group seemed to become much like other Protestant sects in belief, although maintaining many Quaker testimonies and practices, while the other group, although maintaining orthodox Christian beliefs, seemed to be increasingly attached to Quaker traditions. In theological terms, the former group tended to associate the traditional Quaker belief in the Christ Within with orthodox belief in the Holy Spirit, and to rely increasingly on the Scriptures for authority, while the other faction resisted these tendencies. One group came to be associated with an English Friend who traveled in the ministry in America from 1837 to 1840, Joseph John Gurney, and they were labeled "Gurneyites." [13] Gurney was friendly with the church leaders of his day, he was a great Biblical scholar, and his opponents felt he was more of a Protestant than a Quaker.

John Wilbur, a New England school teacher who had first spoken out against Gurney during a visit to England in 1831, felt that true Quaker principles were endangered by

[12] Samuel M. Janney (1801–1880) is best remembered for his biography of William Penn which appeared in 1851. He wrote several other volumes, including a history of Friends which reflected his Hicksite affiliation. He worked for the Negro and was prominent in Indian affairs. H-DQB.

[13] Joseph John Gurney (1788–1847) was a banker in Norwich, the author of many volumes, and the brother of Elizabeth (Gurney) Fry. L-DQB, H-DQB. See also, David E. Swift, *Joseph John Gurney* . . . (Middletown, Conn., 1962).

men like Gurney.[14] In 1845 he and some 500 New England Friends withdrew from New England Yearly Meeting to form their own organization. In 1854 differences within Ohio Yearly Meeting of a similar nature led to splitting that group into a Gurneyite body and a Wilburite yearly meeting, the two being virtually equal in size.

London Yearly Meeting decided once again, but only after prolonged deliberations, that it must choose to recognize a single body, the so-called Gurneyites, and not communicate with the other. Dublin Yearly Meeting, and the other Orthodox bodies in America reached the same decision, with one exception. Philadelphia Yearly Meeting was badly divided on the question, for a sizable group was sympathetic with the Wilburite element in Ohio, and others wished to be allied with the Gurneyites. Furthermore, if Philadelphia did recognize the Wilburite group it would be estranged from other Orthodox bodies. Over a period of time Philadelphia reached the decision that it could only maintain unity by ending the exchange of epistles with all other yearly meetings, and by isolating itself from other bodies.

In the 1860's midwestern Friends were caught up in the revival movement which was sweeping through the other denominations. Quakers often called their sessions "general meetings," but the manner of holding them, the spirit which was developed, and the end results were the same as in revivals in other churches. Instead of worshiping on the basis of silence there was much speaking, and instead of the calm of a traditional meeting these sessions were highly emotional. Music of the kind heard in revivals was introduced, and the altar calls and other revival practices to persuade attenders to make decisions for Christ were used. Walter Robson experienced meetings of this sort in

14 John Wilbur (1774–1856) of Hopkinton, Rhode Island. H-DQB, L-DQB.

several of the yearly meetings he attended, especially when David Updegraff was present.

The innovations which were an integral part of "general meetings" deeply disturbed some Friends. They believed that the revival movement was destroying true Quakerism, and feared that Friends were becoming just another protestant denomination. On the other hand, the Quakers who warmly embraced the revival movement, as well as new converts brought into the meetings through this effort, had little understanding of, or appreciation for the traditional ways of Friends. There was a third group in the middle, those who recognized the contributions of this new movement, but maintained a strong attachment to traditional Quaker ways. This may well have been the largest of the three factions, but it was not always able to have its way, nor was it able to interpret the other two groups to one another. The pressures from the two extremes led to two separations in 1877, when a small conservative minority withdrew from the rest of the yearly meeting, both in Iowa and in Western Yearly Meeting in Indiana, despite efforts of the moderates to hold Friends together.

This middle position is well illustrated by Barnabas Hobbs in a message he delivered in London Yearly Meeting in 1878, when that body was discussing what it should do when faced with two epistles, each claiming to have been sent from *the* Western Yearly Meeting with which it had been in correspondence.[15]

Now, out West, in our part of the earth, many have been brought into the truth by new feelings, and it is in the very nature of things that under these circumstances there should be at first some excitement, and some things are said and done which tend to throw a burden and anxiety on other minds who are more soberly inclined. But, friends, there has been a great upheaval in the land, and the Lord has been in it, and men and women, and children too, have

---

[15] *British Friend* **36** (1878): p. 140. Further discussion of this development may be found in Errol T. Elliott's *Quakers on the American Frontier* (Richmond, Indiana, 1969).

been converted by hundreds. You cannot understand it here—no one can without seeing it. Our meetings were shaken as by a vast whirlwind, until the very atmosphere seemed alive—there was such a power passing through them. When this power had somewhat subsided the effects of it remained; there were the ministers and elders and overseers with the fruits of the revival left flourishing before them, and what were they to do with it? They could not all at once regulate all this young earnest life, and the ministers and elders meet together and consult what to do with all these—these young earnest teachers and others. Then some perhaps disappoint the hopes promised by their first conversion and slip back, and others cool down to what they were before; and others run ahead too fast, and get carried beyond themselves in their liberty and eagerness, and saying and doing wrong things. Hence some Friends set themselves in opposition to it and denounced it all. But, friends, we know that there is something there which the Lord has sent, and we have to take care of it; and when we see persons doing things which would not be approved of everywhere in our meetings, we don't get up and denounce them, but we labour with them after-wards privately, and perhaps they see their mistake; or perhaps in some cases they are disposed to think their opinions right, and we have to wait and pray until they tone down, and become finally united in fellowship. This, of course, is all a work of time, and hence we found that some Friends had not got the patience and forbear-ance to wait while the work progressed, but, to our great grief, finally said they could stand it no longer, and so withdrew. So many of our elders and overseers have left our meetings, and seek to find true worship in going on in the old quiet way they did before the revival. Western Yearly Meeting would fain have had it otherwise, but they could not help it. The power of the revival was more than they could regulate all at once, and you should have been at West-ern Yearly Meeting and heard the prayers and seen the tears on their behalf.

Walter Robson tended to associate himself with the mid-dle group, and certainly made every effort to prevent the schisms which developed in Iowa and Western Yearly Meetings while he was present. His pleas for unity brought severe criticism from some of the so-called "progressive" leaders who told him he "was 'encouraging a spirit they wanted to crush,' and that all *they* did was by Divine command, and therefore must be right." Writing many years later, Robson said, "That word *'crush'* explains much of the spirit of Separation in the U.S.A." [16] But criticism from one extreme did not save Robson from denunciation from the opposite side, for the conservative element disliked his evangelical emphasis, and tried to counteract his influence in Kansas Yearly Meeting and elsewhere.

During the deliberations of London Yearly Meeting in 1878 regarding the two epistles from the separate Western Yearly Meetings, Walter Robson proposed that a deputation be sent to America with the hope that the schism could be healed.[17] This suggestion was adopted, and J. Bevan Braithwaite, Joseph John Dymond, Richard Littleboy, and George Tatham were asked to undertake this service.[18] Although these ministers were unable to bring about a reunion, they did make a helpful contribution to American Quakerism, and when other schisms developed, similar delegations were named. London Yearly Meeting made it clear that they went not as superiors, but as from "one co-ordinate Church to another equally independent, united in a relationship strictly fraternal, in which the only authority is that of love." [19]

---

[16] *British Friend*, N.S., **22** (1913): p. 288. This material, as well as the long quotation from Barnabas Hobbs may also be found in Edward Grubb, *Separations, Their Causes and Effects* . . . (London, 1914).

[17] *British Friend* **36** (1878): p. 129.

[18] London Y.M. *Proceedings*, 1878: pp. 22, 23. J. Bevan Braithwaite (1818–1905), Joseph John Dymond (1825–1907), Richard Littleboy (1819–1895), and George Tatham (1815–1892), were all seasoned Friends, on the average more than twenty years older than Robson, and prominent in yearly meeting affairs. Littleboy described their experiences in "Notes on a Visit to the Yearly Meetings of Friends in Western America," *Friends Quarterly Examiner* **13** (1879): pp. 276–292; and there are also observations in *J. Bevan Braithwaite* (London, [1909]). There are biographical sketches of all four men in L-DQB.

[19] London Y.M. *Proceedings*, 1878: pp. 22, 23; 1879: pp.13–20. One indication of the sympathy for the conservative Friends is found in an unsigned letter in the *British Friend*: "From certain recent examples of advanced Western views and practices, made manifest even on this side of the Atlantic by American visitors, many English Friends will have been prepared, in considerable degree, to sympathize with the minority in their earnest desire for peace, for rest, and for spiritual worship." **36** (1878): p. 113.

Another issue which was being discussed among American Friends in 1877 was the practice of employing a minister to assist a local meeting, especially where a number of new converts had been added. George Fox had denounced the "hireling ministry," as he called it, in the seventeenth century, and Friends had consistently maintained a strong testimony against a professional clergy or special training for those whose gift in the ministry was recognized.

London Yearly Meeting, in the 1875 Supplement to its *Book of Discipline* said, "The work of the ministry of the Gospel is not limited to any particular class or order of men; neither is worship dependent upon the presence of an outward minister." [20] Walter Robson agreed fully with this position, and found himself in a somewhat embarrassing position as he participated in American yearly meetings where this testimony was being modified or abandoned.

In five of the seven yearly meetings he attended, when the queries were answered, the replies reflected the traditional position. Ohio Yearly Meeting said, "We are concerned to maintain our testimony in favor of a Free Gospel Ministry . . ." Western, Kansas, Baltimore, and North Carolina Yearly Meetings made similar statements, but with the exception of Baltimore, the matter was under discussion at least privately, if not openly.[21]

Iowa Yearly Meeting had stopped making a statement against the paid ministry in 1874, and the following year made provision for pastors in a revision of the *Book of Discipline*. Indiana Yearly Meeting had last expressed support for the testimony "against priest's and minister's

---

[20] Pp. 7, 8, in a section entitled, "Ecclesiastical Usurpation."

[21] *Minutes of the Ohio Yearly Meeting of Friends*, 1877: p. 6. Western Yearly Meeting recorded, "Friends appear to bear testimony against priests' and ministers' wages . . .," *Minutes*, p. 16; Kansas, "Friends appear to maintain a testimony against priests' and ministers' wages . . .," *Minutes*, p. 10; Baltimore, "We believe our testimony to a free gospel ministry is generally maintained," *Minutes*, p. 8; North Carolina, "Friends are said to bear a testimony to a free Gospel ministry," *Minutes*, p. 12.

wages . . ." in 1875, and was in the process of revising its *Book of Discipline*.[22]

When the subject came up in Western Yearly Meeting, Walter Robson spoke at length upon the subject, supporting the ancient testimony of Friends against a "hireling ministry." However, his choice of words led some of the Quakers to believe that he was, in fact, supporting the new developments, and the editor of the *Christian Worker*, Daniel Hill, quoted him extensively in a subsequent issue of that journal.[23] He was quoted as having said, "If a man undertake the solemn responsibility of the Ministry of the Gospel, *not* from the constraining love of Christ, but as a means of getting a living then *he* is truly a 'hireling minister.'" He added,

But when a man, called by the Head of the church to preach his Gospel, gives up all his time to it, we have no right to call him a hireling minister, even if he receive one or two thousand dollars. . . . If a minister, full of love to Jesus, and called to the work of the ministry *by the Holy Ghost,* gives up all his time to the work (be he a Friend, or any other name among Christians), surely it is the church's bounded duty to support him, and if need be, his wife and family too.

He went on to comment on the origin of the Friends testimony, saying it "was probably against that compulsory payment of ministers, which was the law in England, till very lately, by which law we had our furniture and goods seized for church rates, year after year." He added that many men had taken parishes for the income, "unconverted men, even bad living men, just because of the yearly income which it yields; such are truly hireling ministers—they care not for the flock." Perhaps without realizing it, he had placed himself squarely in the middle of a controversy which is still alive today.

[22] See the *Minutes* of these two yearly meetings, 1864 to 1877.
[23] **7** (1877): p. 615.

As we read this journal today, we are struck with the sanctimonious tone of the author. When on shipboard, traveling with strangers, he wrote, "I feel I have little I am called to do on board *directly* in a religious direction, but I have been helped much in turning the conversation to a serious strain so that our many hours of leisure I feel are not wasted time." When the ship captain took the passengers up on the bridge, just at sunset, he says, "I began singing 'Praise God from whom all blessings flow,' & it was caught up & sung by the whole company of us, I believe."

During his travels among Friends he wrote constantly of his efforts to be completely faithful to the spirit, to use every opportunity for the glory of God. When he had a slight illness on reaching Ohio, he wrote, "the Lord would thus teach me to bring under my body & bring it into subjection that I should eat to the glory of God." It is not only what he says, but the manner in which it is said that seems strange to us.

We must remember that he was writing in the heyday of the Victorian period, and that he did not sound peculiar or sanctimonious to his contemporaries. One of the great political figures of the era was William E. Gladstone (1809–1898) of whom it was said, he approached moral questions "rather as a clergyman than a layman." Another quotation from a biographical sketch claimed that "From the straight line of orthodox Christianity he never swerved by the breadth of a hair." [24]

Robson was an enthusiast, one who felt strongly about things, a man who was caught up in whatever he was doing. He gently chided the Americans for exaggerating, but he was not entirely free from this weakness himself.

The suspension bridge over the Ohio, at Cincinnati, was "the largest in the world," while the bridge over the Mississippi at St. Louis was "the grandest bridge in the world."

[24] *Dictionary of National Biography*, Suppl., **2**: pp. 281–329.

The park in Baltimore was "one of the loveliest in America," and Cleveland, Ohio, was "one of the prettiest cities I ever saw." Needless to say, Niagara Falls called forth every superlative.

When Western Yearly Meeting liberated Barnabas Hobbs to travel in Europe, he exclaimed, "I never heard so full an expression of unity," and when Indiana Yearly Meeting gave its blessing to R. W. Douglas, for travel to Australasia, he wrote once again, "I never saw so full an expression of unity." Persons who thanked Robson for his messages were almost invariably "much too kind" in what they said, and he often felt "more than usually blessed" in what he had been led to say in meetings.

Walter Robson was somewhat overwhelmed with the response which his presence and messages brought in the various yearly meetings. At Richmond, Indiana, local photographers took his picture in order to sell copies to those at yearly meeting. In Baltimore he wrote, "I never knew anything like the love & unity heaped on me here, . . . I can & do most surely feel & know it is the Lord's work & not mine." He was taken to meet the President of the United States, Rutherford B. Hayes, he was asked to give the keynote sermon at North Carolina Yearly Meeting, and preached to crowds of 5,000 on yearly meeting Sundays in some places. It is to his credit that he remained modest about his own abilities, and gave God the glory for what was accomplished.

Robson accepted the Americans in a remarkably open manner. He formed warm friendships, expressed great appreciation for much that he saw, and was clearly delighted with his experiences among Friends in the United States. Considering it was the fashion for overseas visitors to ridicule and denounce American customs and ideas, he was most positive in his responses and comments. Quaker visitors among their fellow religionists in America were generally more understanding than their contemporaries.

In the beginning of the journal he was sometimes critical of Americans, the way they spoke, the use of chewing tobacco, or the exuberance of the Friends in Ohio. This tone disappeared after a time, but a slightly patronizing phrase continued to appear. When it turned a bit cool on September 18 in Plainfield, and two large fires were started in the meetinghouse, Robson commented, "The dear Friends here seem fearfully afraid of being cold." This phrase, "The dear Friends" was used many times in describing actions which he did not understand, or thought odd.

He was by no means as tolerant of Friends whose doctrines he considered unsound. He seemed to know instinctively when Hicksites were present in public meetings, and would preach at them, pointing out the errors of their ways. There is no indication in the journal that he ever met any Hicksites informally, or became acquainted with any personally.

He was also critical of those who held what he called "Wilburite" ideas, but he did not assume the same uncompromising stance toward them. While he thought they were mistaken in doctrine, he was not prepared to read them out of the Society of Friends. He willingly differed with them in public, but was also open to conversations with them in private. He was genuinely fond of some of them, and opposed the efforts to force them out of the existing yearly meetings. In Ohio he "felt constrained to pray for the separated body [the Wilburites] as well as the sound Friends."

When the Yearly Meeting on Ministry and Oversight met in London on Tuesday afternoon, May 21, 1878, a considerable period of time was given to listening to a report from Walter Robson on his experiences the previous year. The *British Friend* said that "His narrative was both interesting and instructive, for the brief period during which he

was on that Continent embraced an extensive service." [25]
This example of British understatement contrasts with Robson's own method of expressing himself, but it may be a
fitting conclusion to this introduction even so.

[25] **36** (1878): p. 125.

THE JOURNAL OF WALTER ROBSON

I. Voyage Across the Atlantic

After fervent prayer only interrupted by many blinding tears, I took a loving farewell of my precious wife & our five darling children on the morning of 3rd day 8th mo. 7th 1877 & accompanied by my beloved Father drove to Audley End station, leaving my dear Mother-sister Priscie & brother J. J. R. watching me from my garden.[1] Had two hours to wait at Peterborough in a soaking rain, after which we proceeded to Huddersfield where cousin Joshua W. Robson met us at the station & escorted us in a cab to Uncle Isaac Robson's where a warm welcome awaited us. Spent a quiet evening there in which my thoughts often assumed the character of earnest prayer for the very dear ones I had left at home, mingled with solemn thoughts of the work I am expecting so soon to enter on in America.

4th day 8th Dear Uncle prayed beautifully for me & my beloved partner in life, that she might be kept in perfect peace, her mind stayed on God continually. I felt comforted & strengthened. Called on cousins J. & T. & saw some of their dear children.[2] Father & Uncle took leave of me at the station, Cousin Joshua very kindly going with me to Liverpool. Much enjoyed the beautiful scenery we passed on the way—water & mountains in rich variety & in full summer foliage. Dined at the station at Liverpool & having a few spare minutes, went into St. George's hall and saw Judge Hawkins trying a case. Then took a cab to Prince's Landing Stage where we found two Steam Tugs, one to convey passengers & the other their luggage on board our transatlantic steamship. It was cheering to meet Joseph

---

[1] Audley End was the railway station on the main line from London to Cambridge most convenient to Saffron Walden. "Priscie" was an older, unmarried sister, Rachel Priscilla, and "J.J.R." was Joseph John Robson (1828–1914).

[2] Joshua Wheeler Robson (1831–1917), and Thomas Robson (1836–1920).

FIG. 1. Walter Robson, his wife Christina and their five children in 1878.

& Isabella Jones of Chicago, their daughters Francis & Maria (Frank & Ida) & our dear friend Hannah Thistlethwaite, all going as passengers with me.[3] Reached the "Pennsylvania" at about 4 p.m. & soon the gong sounded for all who were not passengers to go on shore, so I took leave of Joshua, but owing to low tide it was 6:30 before our big engines began their work & slowly screwed us down the river. It was a calm quiet evening, but inclined to be wet so I sat with the Jones's in a nice "little house on deck," at top of the companion staircase, where we had much converse till bed time. Wrote to my beloved Christina & joined in some Sankey's Hymns, turning into bed at 11:30.

The quiet did not last long & it soon began to blow fresh & in our teeth, so that when the gong sounded for breakfast on the morning of 5th day 8 mo. 9th out of about 40 Saloon passengers we only mustered six or seven. I feel it cause for real & earnest thankfulness that I still maintain my charac-

[3] Joseph Jones (1815?–1889) was an elder in Chicago Monthy Meeting, and W. R. later visited them in their home. *Friends Review* **42** (1889): p. 704.

ter as a good sailor, never sea-sick, so that I was able to day to enjoy the rolling & pitching as we passed along in full view of the beautiful coast of Ireland. At about 3 P.M. we steamed into Queenstown Harbour,[4] waiting there till a Steam tug brought us several passengers, some rather rough looking ones for Stearage, & two jolly Priests of the Roman Church as Saloon companions—one of them very nearly 7 feet high & big in proportion. I sent two letters on shore, one to acknowledge a telegram brought me from my dear wife, containing brighter tidings than in my little faith I had dared to hope for. We soon sped again on our way & now expect to see no more land till we reach the North American continent. The fellow occupant of my state room is a Doctor Palma who has just been at the seat of war, where he went to inspect the various arrangements for the care of the poor wounded soldiers on both sides. He witnessed (side by side with Grant, the Daily News correspondent) the bombardment of Nicopolis & had a slight wound from a bombshell while watching the awful scene at night.[5] I have had a greal deal of converse with J. Jones, a man of much thought & an advanced Christian. I am thankful for his counsel & sympathy. Kept very near the Irish coast till near midnight we passed Cape Clear, & now we have only the beautiful circle of the ocean round us. Even the sea-birds which surrounded us in hundreds, have all gone back to shore again.

6th day 8th mo. 10th. A lovely day at sea but blowing hard & so cold that I was glad to wear my thick Ulster coat. We seem to have very few English people on board, the vessel being an American liner. Americans like to patronize her & out of more than 200 passengers fore & aft, I do not know of more than ½ a dozen of my fellow country-

[4] Now called Cobh, near Cork.
[5] Nicopolis, now Nikopol, is in northern Bulgaria. The town was captured on July 15, 1877.

men. The smoking & chewing are incessant & the smoking room is the best & most comfortable part of the ship.[6] This afternoon we witnessed a very interesting performance such as I never saw before, the drilling of the fire brigade which takes place every voyage to be certain that all is ready in case of that worst of all catastrophes a fire at sea! On this vessel every seaman & officer-steward Engineer cabin boy &c has his post of duty as a fire brigade man & at the sharp ringing of all the bells this afternoon in a marvellously short time (say 3 min.) our ten boats were all swung over the ship's side, ready any moment to be lowered, the pumps were manned, rows of men with buckets, others with hatchets & others with "patent extinguishers" &c, &c. The ship seems every way well managed & I feel well satisfied I have selected this Line for my two voyages & that H. Balkwill & the Pumphreys are coming by same Line. Every day at 11 o'clock the Captain and Doctor make a minute examination of every cabin to see that it is thoroughly pure & well ventilated, clean everywhere. My dearest Tenie will know how greatly that is needed on ship board.

7th day 8th mo. 11th. A soaking wet & windy day, keeping the ladies below stairs & making the smoking room the only available place of comfort. But one learns very much from the association with men of culture & position belonging to another nation. It is amusing how *very* highly they all talk of the United States & their great superiority in every way over the old country. But we have some good people on board, one noble looking gentleman who confessed to us how greatly he had been blessed by Mrs. Pearsall Smith, another a Roman Catholic, Mr. Shiel from Cork, came over with C. Talbot & was much blessed by her labours on board & in Cork. I feel I have little I am called

---

[6] The chewing of tobacco, accompanied by spitting out the juice, was always a great trial to English visitors among Americans.

to do on board *directly* in a religious direction, but I have
been helped much in turning the conversation to a serious
strain so that our many hours of leisure I feel are not wasted
time. It is fixed to day that the services tomorrow shall be
conducted in the morning by the Revd Dr. Watson (Episcopal) & in the evening by the Revd Dr. Harper (Presbyterian) so I shall only form one of the audience probably.

1st day 8th mo. 12th. A heavy gale from the North—such
a change, no one hardly at breakfast, all portholes screwed
tight, the skylights in the Saloon boarded up & covered
with canvas to prevent the seas which are breaking over
us from smashing the glass. My wife knows how great is
the unsettlement on ship board occasioned by a heavy gale.
No one is able to read, write, or hardly to think collectedly.
Dr. Watson ill in his bunk, quite unable to take the service,
the Saloon dark & dismal, so that a service there would be
impossible & all but about 6 of us are ill in bed. Spent most
of the day in the smoking room, the deck being unsafe
from the constant seas washing over it. Dinner was served
as well as could be under the circumstances, but of course
tidiness was out of the question. We hoped however that
after tea Dr. Harper would be able to preach in the Saloon,
but he announced himself, too ill, so, to my surprise, a
gentleman Mr. Bodean (a friend of E. P. Gurney's) asked
the Captain to request me to conduct a simple service.[7]
This I was thankful to do & we had a blessed time. A Mr.
Beck (organist to a large church in Philadelphia) hung on
to the Piano somehow & our good Commander, Captain
Harris led the Hymns. We sang "Jesus, Saviour of my Soul,"
then I read 17th John & Dr. Harper prayed. We sang "Oh
for a closer walk with God," & I spoke for about ½ an hour
from the words "This is life eternal &c." I had to cling with
my arms around an iron pillar to keep from falling. Sung

---

[7] Eliza Paul (Kirkbride) Gurney (1801–1881), widow of Joseph John Gurney,
who lived near Burlington, N. J., where W. R. visited her in November. H-DQB.

"Sun of my soul," & I closed with prayer. Those in their cabins heard me & I received far too much in the way of thanks—Dr. Watson & Dr. Harper especially, but I do feel very thankful that after all my blessed Saviour had a little service for me & gave me the needful help to perform it.

2nd day 13th. Such a change again! The gale all gone, every port opened & quite a gay scene on deck of ladies & gentlemen reading & playing games. All the Jones's are on deck & I hear poor dear H. T. means to come up. We have not seen her since we left Queenstown. How my thoughts live with the precious ones I have left at home & the last Sunday at home & to day the last day at home last week. It seems a *very* long six days since I took that sad sad farewell of all I most love on earth & all who make my home so sweet. I hope I may escape the constant nasal twang that all Americans seem to have. I detest it but I fear it comes on one quite unconsciously. I have asked the Jones's who have it *very* strongly & they say they see a great difference between their own & our delivery, but are unconscious of any peculiarity in themselves. We are making splendid runs every day. 327 304 302 are the result of the past three days. I long that I had been able to bring my dear wife to England in a ship as clean & luxurious as this is. We verily "fare sumptuously every day" & the water is all iced. The lettuces & are all preserved in ice & are as fresh as if just cut from ones own garden. We have clean towels every day & clean sheets to day.

3rd day 14th. A week of my separation from home is over & now I am hoping Arthur and Mary are getting near England but fancy they would get the same gale we had so severely on 1st day.[8] Dear H. T. on deck to day. I gave her my arm as long as she could walk, but her week of

---

[8] Arthur Midgley (1852–1919) had gone out to Australia, where he met and married Mary Doncaster Cox, sister of W.R.'s wife Christina, and now returned with her as a bride to live near the Robsons in Saffron Walden. L-DOB.

sickness has made her very shaky. I have been all over the foreport of the ship to day inspecting the steerage &. Most of or all the forecabin passengers are Roman Catholics. Poor things! they are dreadfully huddled together, but even there, everything is thoroughly inspected every day & is as clean as possible. Four of our passengers on this ship came home with Stanley Pumphrey. I fancy him & Sarah & H. Balkwill taking leave of their homes to day. We have reached a part of the ocean to day where there is almost always a thick fog—the great Bank of Newfoundland. The water is comparatively shallow, & the fog horn snorting constantly to warn any vessels, which may be near, of our approach. The weather is cold, the deck clammy & wet, a current from the Northern ice fields has set in, but the sea is very smooth. As evening approached the fog grew more & more dense. I believe we could not see a ships length in any direction, so the captain was on the look out all the time & the fog-horn blown every three minutes making a noise to be heard for miles. Our passengers were nervous & of course there is serious danger both from icebergs & the very probable approach of other vessels, but through the care of Him to whom the darkness & the light are both alike, we were unharmed. In the evening Dr. Harper gave us a very interesting lecture on California, the Yosemite Valley, San Francisco, &.

4th day 15th. The sea calm as a river & every one seeming to fulfill the words of the Psalmist, "Then are they glad because they be quiet," as the result of the statement, "He maketh the storm a calm, so that the waves thereof are still." With the exception of one man who is fast drinking himself to death, I never voyaged with a more intelligent or respectable set of people, never saw so little strong drink imbibed, but the chewing & smoking last from 6 in the morning till midnight. Just before teatime our engines stopped owing to some part of the machinery breaking &

the cessation of the vibration had a most peculiar effect on us all. To night Dr. Watson read prayers & preached from the words "Abba - Father," but I have yet to learn to enjoy written sermons. The Prayer book of the American Episcopal Church is very similar to ours but by no means identical, & the good Dr. took great liberties with it this evening. Our engines remained stationary most of the night but we are full "steamahead" this morning.

5th day 16th. Going through another dense fog & everything is very damp and sticky. I have been talking to our head steward who has had a remarkable history, having been twice shipwrecked. The 1st time he was on board the ship Arctic, on which I think my dear parents will remember that in 1854, our friends from America, Mahlon Day & his wife embarked for the United States, yielding to their friends advice to go, while feeling very uneasy in their own minds about it.[9] They were drowned, & the steward tells me he well remembers the last time he saw M. Day, he was in his broad brimmed hat floating about in the sea on his mattrass.

6th day 8th mo. 17th. To day has been a very variable one, lovely sun shine, then thick fogs & at night it blew a gale of wind. We seem now to have left the region of gales & cold & it is a perfectly exquisite day, quite hot & set me longing to have my Tenie & our darlings with me, to enjoy the calm sea, the Porpoises, Sea birds and vessels around us. Just before sunset Captain Harris asked us all, up on to the bridge where all passengers are forbidden to go, as they steer the ship &c. from that elevated position. The scene was most lovely, almost tropical. I began singing "Praise God from whom all blessings flow," & it was caught up & sung by the whole company of us, I believe. After

[9] Mahlon Day (1790–1854) was a Quaker printer and bookseller who specialized in children's books. His wife was English, and they were crossing the Atlantic to visit her family. H-DQB.

tea, Dr. Palmer gave us a very interesting lecture on the
Turko-Russian war. We had several of the forecabin passengers with us to hear it. Once more a dense fog & the
horn snorting every few minutes about midnight.

7th day 8th mo. 18th. We hope to get to Philadelphia
tomorrow & are making a splendid run. Several have re-
marked to me that they never voyaged with so many serious
people before. I have not heard one coarse or bad word,
or seen any strong drink drunk except in cases of sickness,
perhaps with *one* exception & that an Englishman from
Oldham. To day we have seen a whale spouting at a little
distance off the ship. Every one is on deck and it is too hot
to take much exercise. This morning, the Captain asked
any of us who inclined, to visit the engine rooms. I did
so & was much pleased with our grand propelling power,
but the heat in the furnace room was awful.

After tea we assembled in the Saloon & I gave a little
sketch of the South Pacific & Australia. I tried to stop, but
was ordered by the Captain to "go on & never mind the
clock." My kind fellow passengers received me very cordially & I ventured to introduce several points of Christian
truth (to improve the occasion) especially prayer & to my
great surprise Father Prendagast (the big Priest) thanked
me very cordially. After I had finished the Captain said,
they had found a "stowaway" in a tub & he would be
brought before us. A tub was produced & Mr. Davies, one
of our passengers, proved to be a first rate ventriloquist &
the thing passed off excellently well. The stewardess was
so completely taken in, that she still believes there was
a man in the tub, & that he *was* sent out to sea through a
porthole. I was much amused by a little episode to day.
We had to give our tickets to the Purser & enter our names
& addresses in a large book kept for the purpose. On looking though the book afterwards, I saw "D. D." clearly
affixed to my name. At first I felt really annoyed, thinking

it a foolish piece of impertinence, but spoke to the Captain about it, & carefully erased it. He replied, "I did it sir, for the passengers told me you were too modest even to call yourself, "Reverend," so I said "I would fix it up for you." I told him I was *not* a Doctor of Divinity. He said, "I guess you are quite as much as any of them."

1st day 8th mo. 19th. What a contrast since last Sunday! then a heavy gale & now a calm, bright summer day, very hot. We are now steaming up Delaware Bay with our Pilot on board. The banks about as flat and sandy as can be, but Cape May City, Sea-grove &c. are pretty, from their long rows of fine hotels. As we proceeded, the river Delaware became narrower & more picturesque, New Jersey State on one side & Delaware State the other. At 11 o'clk we assembled on the deck & had a closing service, conducted by Dr. Harper, sang "Rock of Ages," and he read portions of Scripture, sang "Nearer my God, to Thee." & he preached from the words, "There shall be no more Sea." It was strikingly appropriate to the closing of our voyage. I closed in prayer & we sang, "Sweet by & bye." Dr. Harper spoke of our all agreeing we had never so pleasant a company to voyage together, before, & tho' we have only been 11 days together, there are many of us feel the parting as quite a sorrowful one. I have received several pressing invitations to visit, if I have time in Philadelphia while waiting for a ship on my return from North Carolina. At Chester the health officer came on board & we had all to pass in review before him. He gave us a clean bill of health. Then came the Custom House Officers, a dozen or more. This is a great improvement on our English plan, as while the men searched our boxes, we were steaming ahead all the while. They are very strict, nothing avails to prevent every package being opened & closely searched. The reason is that so many people buy jewelry, silks & other dutiable articles in England & Paris, & try to get them home unpaid. Finally

at 6 o'clk, we slowly moved up to the wharf; I was touched
to watch the many warm greetings, Parents & children,
brothers & sisters, husband & wife, as we set foot on North
American shores. The Jones's had their son & son in law
to meet them & Dr. Rhoads (Editor of the Friends Review)
met me, he is Mary Haines's brother. I was pleased to see
Edward Skull (Rufus King's companion when he came first
to England).[10] E. Skull took H. Thistlethwaite with him to
Anna Potts'. My fellow voyagers did not forget to shake
hands with me very warmly, & one old lady who I know
very little of thanked me for the good I had done her, but I
was so surprised at it, I knew not what to say. Dr. Rhoads
took me in a carriage through the streets of this great city
(900,000 inhabitants) to a station whence trains run to
the suburbs. Thence "took the cars" to German Town
(9 miles) to his pretty residence. Now I long extremely
to have my precious wife here. The weather is just perfect,
about 100 in the shade, full summer heat, clear & bright,
& the rich flowers (hothouse in England) are blooming
in the gardens in all their luxuriance. On our supper table
was such a dish of peaches as I have never seen since I
left "Summer Hill." The railway trains are most foreign,
the carriages are approached by a flight of steps at one
end, & the seats are short ones holding only two each
against the window. A long aisle occupying the centre of
the carriages. At one end is a large filter of iced water &
glasses, all gratis. Enjoyed a night in a comfortable bed
under mosquito curtains.

2nd day 8th mo. 20th. A cold bath was a luxury this
morning after little chance of a good wash since I left
home. After reading Dr. R. & I offered prayer. He very
especially praying for great blessings on my work in this
land & adding, "this we pray, not in fear but in undoubted

---

[10] Edward L. Scull (1846–1884), a Philadelphia wool merchant who had gone
to England in 1876 as a companion to Rufus King. H-DQB.

confidence it will be so." We then went into Town again by rail, calling on Mary Nicholson & to a brokers to change English gold into American paper. Home to dinner at which meal water melons formed a great part. I cannot understand the nasal twang of everybody. Even the steam engines have it, & instead of the shrill whistle of our english ones, make a noise like a man blowing his nose. They carry a great bell & as they move along through the streets without any protection, the bell tolls dismally to warn passers by to get out of the way. We visited the Hall of Independence of British authority. Outside is a colossal statue of William Penn & with in, are original letters of his own writing & the original painting by West, of "Penn's treaty with the Indians."

I have decided to leave here tomorrow & take the cars for Ohio, lodging tomorrow night at Altoona & getting to Mount Pleasant on 4th day evening. I long to hear from home, & I long for my dearest ones to hear of me. I may report myself quite well, though of course feeling the intense heat. Think of me & pray for me. Remember the time here is five hours behind yours, so that when it is your bedtime, I am about 5 o'clk in the afternoon. I must close this now, so that I can post it before I leave for the West. May every rich blessing rest always on you all, my dear ones at home, so prays, every day, your loving friend,

Walter Robson

Much love to all enquiring friends of my own meeting, or elsewhere, at discretion.

II. To Ohio Yearly Meeting

2nd day 8th mo. 20th 1877. Dr. Rhodes accompanied me to the Post Office, where I posted my first budget for home.[1] Met a real live Colorado Beetle & killed him on the spot, he was the facsimile of the model J. J. R. showed us the day before I left. We called on Hettie Clibborn daughter of Joseph Shewell of Darlington & had a very warm greeting from her. She is living in a very comfortable little house, has one baby & seems very happy. Inspected the meeting house premises. German Town meeting has over 200 members. Yardley Warner has belonged to it, but has recently been deposed from his station of Minister & recommended to England.[2] In the evening we had a nice interesting call from Anthony Kimber who travelled several weeks with uncle I. R. & has a loving remembrance of my revered Grandparents.[3]

3rd day 21st. Dr. Rhodes & I went to breakfast at A. Kimber's, his brother in law James Whitall joined us there. J. W. is own brother to dear Hannah W. Smith & he & A. Kimber married daughters of Marmaduke Cope.[4] M. C. lives next door, but in common with most Philadelphia Friends is now away at the seaside. Before breakfast A. Kimber & I prayed & then he simply offered to go with me as my companion to Ohio. I feel very thankful it is so. He leaves a wife in extremely delicate health, a confirmed

---

[1] "Budget" is used here to mean a bundle of news.

[2] Yardley Warner (1815–1885), was active in the effort to aid the Freedmen after the Civil War. He was considered too evangelical by Philadelphia Friends. See Stafford Allen Warner, *Yardley Warner, The Freedman's Friend* (Didcot, Engl., [1957]).

[3] Isaac Robson, the uncle he visited in Huddersfield on the way to Liverpool. His grandparents, Elizabeth (Stephenson) and Thomas Robson, who traveled in America together in 1838. L-DQB.

[4] Marmaduke Cope (1804–1897) an elder in Twelfth Street Meeting in Philadelphia, gave his time to philanthropic work, and his home was frequently open to overseas visitors. H-DQB.

invalid & has telegraphed to her (to Newport where she is staying with M. Cope) & only awaits tidings of her state, before he joins me at the station to journey two days to Ohio.

Dr. Rhodes afterwards accompanied me into Philadelphia through which we rode in a horse car (tram omnibus we call them in England). Went through some of the finest parts of this great City & greatly admired the Churches & other public buildings. The Episcopal Churches here are nothing so fine as those of other denominations. At the station met A. K. & we took the Cars for Altoona. It is a curious new experience after a few miles, a man walks through the train selling peaches & pears. Another follows with Magazines, another with sensation Novels, while a fourth bellows out the name of the next station we stop at, as for instance "the next station is Harrisburgh. Passengers for Columbia & the North change there, Passengers for Pittsburgh are allowed 20 min. for dinner." It being 3:30 P.M. we availed ourselves of the dinner. In the dining room of Harrisburgh depot, each person sits down to a table & before each is placed a little dish of potatoes, another of cabbage, one each of sweet potatoe, green corn & tomato. Then comes peach pie & water melon, for this sumptuous repast we pay 75 cents, including hot meat, of course. Our journey was a very lovely one, through miles of waving maize & tobacco plants & then alongside & over the river Susquehannah for, I suppose, 50 miles—the river close to us one side & the high hills covered with rich foliage, the other. Then followed the Juniatta river, still more lovely— the hills increasing in height till we reached Altoona, 326 miles west of Philadelphia at 8 P.M. Our Car in the railway was a perfect drawingroom with rich Brussels carpet & furnished entirely with velvet covered lounging-chairs, each fixed to the floor, but revolving on its own axis, that we could turn first one side & then the other, wherever the scenery was the most charming. One end of our carriage was fitted with washingrooms &c, so that every luxury was ours. Reached Altoona at 8 o'clk & took rooms at the hotel at the station, a first class establishment, & after a tea supper, had a stroll by moonlight, through the town, & then a long conversation, sitting in the verandah.

4th day 22nd. Left Altoona in an observation Car, at the back of the train, put on purposely, to enable travelers to see the beauties we pass through. Three powerful engines pulled us up a very steep incline, richly wooded mountains & deep ravines on all sides of us, & old black tree stumps Australian like. Such is the ascent of the Alleghany mountains. Just at the summit is a tunnel & then a station where the observation car was taken off. The ride continues very lovely, crossing great rivers often tumbling & foaming over rocks & fallen timber till about 2 o'clk we reached the great centre of the coal mining, the city of Pittsburg. I never saw a more dismal sight than that which met our gaze there —the fearful results of the most terrible Railway strike on record.[5] The station, engine houses, workshops &c are all burnt down & I think we saw full 60 locomotives literally burnt up, besides debris of all sorts, 9,000 tons of iron, the remains of engines carriages &c., are now offered for sale. We managed to get a peach dinner at an Inn & then took the Cars again for Portland. At a station about halfway nearly 100 Friends got in, bound (like us) for Ohio Y. Meeting. Our course lay nearly all the way from Pittsburgh close to the Ohio river, a lovely broad stream with pretty little craft sailing over it. At Portland station, a motly group we looked. Dear good simple hearted Friends in cotton Friends Bonnets mantles & dresses—men in Alpacca trowsers & each worn out long ago & nearly 20 vehicles sent over from Mount Pleasant to fetch us. George Jenkins

---

[5] See, Foster Rhea Dulles, *Labor in America* (New York, 1949), pp. 119–121; Samuel Yellen, *American Labor Struggles* (New York, 1956), pp. 16–18.

(the Yearly Meeting clerk) took me in his Buggie with two other Friends 7 miles to his home. The road was dreadful such as no English springs could possibly survive. A lovely drive! my precious wife should have been with us. It was so exceedingly like the road from her dear home to the mountain farm & quite as steep & bad in many places. At G. Jenkins's I am in very comfortable quarters, writing this in a good bedroom all to myself. Here I had a warm welcome from mine hostess Sarah Jenkins & her guests Sarah Satterthwaite & James N. Richardson. Somehow it is pleasant to see home faces in a foreign land! [6] My heart was gladdened by a sweet letter from my dearest wife which has made me thank God & take courage. He has heard my prayers for her, I love so well, & for our sweet lambs.

5th day 8th Mo: 23rd. God disposes of us as He in His love thinks best. I came here expecting to be in readiness to attend Ohio Y. Meeting, but awoke this morning so poorly that I have been in or on my bed all day & as evening went on, became so ill that Sarah Jenkins sent for her brother Dr. Updegraph a very excellent Physician who gave me good medicine & ordered a large mustard plaister. My dear friends have vied with each other who could be kindest & A. Kimber prayed by my side from the words, "Lord, behold he whom thou lovest is sick." After the fever abated I got some sleep, but it has been a very humiliating introduction to the American Yearly Meetings. A lesson of love for me, I know. Possibly I have been regaling too freely on melons & peaches & the Lord would thus teach me to bring under my body & bring it into subjection that I should eat to the glory of God. Several times in the night J.N.R. & G. K. Jenkins came into see after me & the Dr. came at 7 o'clk this morning.

[6] James N. Richardson (1817–1896) was a minister in Ulster Quarterly Meeting of Dublin Yearly Meeting, and active in many Quaker concerns. He returned to America to participate in the Richmond Conference of 1887. L-DQB.

6th day 8th mo: 24th. Yesterday was held a devotional meeting & the opening sitting of Ministers & Elders, at which my certificates were read & this morning the Yearly Meeting began and a mission meeting after it.[7] I felt some what better & went this evening in my host's buggie to the meeting-house to a devotional meeting. My dear friends at home have little idea of an American Friends devotional meeting. The groaning, responding, "Amen! Brother" "God help thee sister," were just kept up all the while. Several hymns were just started by Friends all over the meeting & sung by any who inclined. David Updegraff who is looked on as one of the finest ministers in America presided & near the close, asked all Friends who decided then & there for Christ, to rise—several rose—then for all who wished conversation, & several more rose. Then all who were unconverted & several more stood up. Prayers were offered for each class. A recorded Minister with a certificate from one of the Westerly Y.M.s a negro offered a beautiful prayer.[8] He is a "son of thunder." Mount Pleasant is a little old fashioned township of about 900 inhabitants, a large meeting of Friends who managed among them to board & lodge nearly all the Yearly Meeting. It is only held here every two years, alternating with Damascus. G. K. Jenkins is a farmer, his wife a sister of D. Updegraff & a sweet minister. He has, I think, beside his daughters, one married with her husband & family, about 10 or 12 lodging in the house, but where he puts them all, I cannot think. I dined at D. Updegraff's & went to the 1st day School conference in the afternoon—not a very striking meeting. After tea, the adjourned meeting of Ministers &

[7] The complete list of ministers whose certificates were read included the three overseas Friends, Sarah B. Satterthwaite, James N. Richardson, and Walter Robson; and Thomas Ladd of New York Yearly Meeting, William F. Lewis of Iowa, and Daniel Hill, William G. Hubbard, and Nathan and Esther Frame. *Minutes of the Ohio Yearly Meeting of Friends, 1877.*

[8] William Allen (b.?–1898) was born a slave in Tennessee. He was first a Methodist, and then joined Friends. H-DQB.

Elders, spent throughout in discussing the ground-work of our most holy faith. I think I never attended a more intensely interesting meeting. It lasted till after 10 o'clk & then adjourned till 2nd day night. The fact is, Hicksism has a little hold with a few of the Ministers & Elders of Ohio & hence the necessity of great plainness of speech & great clearness of doctrine & soundness of view, in speaking, writing or preaching of Christ & His atonement. It is very sweet to meet again dear Caroline Talbot who lives here. She looks just as in England—the same clear expressive eyes, pale face & languid air, which we all remember so well, at home. I hope to visit her & Kinsey in a few days. She told me to give her dear love to my dear wife, parents & sister & G. S. & E. G.

7th day 8th Mo: 25th Much better this morning & up to breakfast at 6.30.[9] Went to a meeting of Ministers & Elders at 8 o'clk. The meeting-house is as plain as the one at Coggeshall, only it seats when the shutters are down (as at Coggeshall) 2000 persons, some say, 3000.[10] Our meeting of Ministers & Elders this morning could do no business, there was such a rush of religious exercises, about 26 prayers & preaching interspersed, till the clerk rose & said, we must break up in 5 min. so he just read the opening minute & at once adjourned till tonight. Then a sitting of the Y. Meeting, very lively, the state of the Society considered. J.N.R. & I spoke at some length & a few other Friends. Then the meeting adjourned. A good deal of time was occupied in reading the Answers & summary to the queries 7 in number.

1st day 26th Walked in to attend devotional meeting. I wish my dear ones could just be at one of them. There

---

[9] In the original journal the entry for August 25 was added as a postscript after concluding Sunday, August 26.

[10] Coggeshall was a meeting west of Colchester, and W.R.'s home quarterly meeting of Essex (after 1881 Essex and Suffolk). The meetinghouse referred to was taken down in 1878.

would be nearly 500 present this morning. D. Updegraph has a wonderful gift for managing these great gatherings. I will just give a sort of echo of a little bit of it. "Now Friends, there is not much time, so just begin straight away, 100 of you." "I've got perfect peace—amen bless the Lord"! "I've got my attraction of gravitation reversed." "Praise the Lord for that, help-help-help." "I knew the time when Jesus did not love me." "What's that thee's saying brother"? "No, I mean I remember the time I didn't love Him." "I'm safe in the arms of Jesus" & we sang a verse of it, right off. "He leadeth beside the green pastures, because he has not any that aint green." "I give myself up to Him"—Amen. "I love Him & wish you all, dear friends." "Stop brother! thee must not exhort, only give thy own experience" &c. These meetings are very exercising to me. I almost dread them, & I think you had need pray that I may overcome my too keen sense of the ludicrous. After this meeting had sat nearly two hours, we came out for a short time to air the house, & remove the dividing shutters. Then about 1500 people, Friends & others (leaving over 100 buggies & horses in the adjoining yard), assembled, & we held our meeting for worship. Some one prayed & then some one else began & the people generally, joined in singing, "There is a fountain filled with blood." J. N. Richardson asked for silence, but one Friend (a woman) began to preach on temperance directly, & while she preached another woman was offering prayer in a very loud voice. D. Updegraph then rose & said, he insisted on silence, & he has such power that they obeyed at once. Then I rose & spoke for ¾ of an hour & was greatly blessed. The responding was full enough. Then a dear woman (Mrs. Mathieson) a native of England, followed me for about as long. A few short communications—another hymn & we broke up. Dined at my quarters & met again for worship at 3.p.m. A lady Friend, Esther Frame (very young) spoke for an hour & a half, the most finished wonderful sermon I ever heard, on the words, "made unto us, wisdom righteousness, sanctification & redemption." [11] Tea at Isaac Thomas's & then meeting for worship again. Only about 1000 in the evening. I spoke a long while, followed by J. N. R. & Thomas Ladd (the latter is brother to Isabella Jones).[12] Prayers are so continual here that the practice of rising has been discontinued altogether. Home to bed about 10 o'clk. Dear friends here, are very kind & loving. I am passing through great conflict of mind as to my position here. I feel truly like a dwarf among giants & often the query will come & it fills my eyes with tears. Why should I be away from my precious wife & family & all my dear ones & our business, to attend meetings where surely every additional labourer is more a burden than a help? yet I feel no release from it & I have had (2nd day 8th Mo 22nd) [sic] a sweet talk with dear Sarah Satterthwaite about it. She seems very able to sympathise with me, but truly encouraging. We both feel that the Ohio Y. M. is in a most peculiar position & the question is, "whereunto will this grow"? A Church of earnest labourers, all wanting to preach & pray & sing let loose rejoicing in their freedom & impatient of any control. Well, I love to see life, but I would not for anything see London Yearly Meeting copy from Ohio. This journal leaves me pretty well in health, feeling to need the prayers of all who love me. All that love & kindness can do, is done for me. My love very warmly to you all.

2nd day 8th mo 27th A roasting hot day! so that we were

---

[11] Esther Frame (1840–1920) had been reared a Methodist, but joined Friends because there was opportunity for a woman to minister among Quakers. She and her husband Nathan Frame (1835–1914) were active evangelists from the 1860's on. *Reminiscences of Nathan T. and Esther G. Frame* (Cleveland, Ohio, 1907). H-DQB.

[12] Thomas Ladd (1832–1882) is a younger brother of William Ladd, and like him studied at Haverford, and moved from Ohio to New York to enter business. *Biog. Cat. Haverford; Friends Review* **36** (1883): p. 361.

glad to sit & fan ourselves all meeting time. A. Kimber
has kindly bought me a nice friendly looking fan fit for the
gallery. After an early breakfast (about 6.30 every day)
went to the Meeting for Sufferings, or as it is here called,
the Representative Meeting & passed a very long testimony
concerning Edith Griffiths. It takes ¾ of an hour to read.
It is to be read in the Y. Meeting. At 10 o'clk the Yearly
Meeting sat down & we proceeded with the state of the
Society. Much exercise was expressed as to the suitable
reading for the young & the baneful effects of newspapers.
Then the shutters were removed, so as to join the Women's
Y. Meeting to us & dear Caroline Talbot gave us most
sweetly her account of her visit to England & Ireland, &
returned her certificates. Much unity was expressed & I
was glad to affirm the love & unity felt for her at home.
Then broke up, & I walked out to dinner at Asahel Hussey's,
where was a large concourse of Friends & we had much
spiritual food socially. Back to my quarters to send off
letters for home & then to Meeting to the Committee of
the Boarding-school which had only just been rescued by
law from the Wilbur Y. Meeting when it was burnt down.
It was finally decided to rebuild it, if it be possible to
raise the money, & John Butler & George K. Jenkins are
set apart to visit the Easterly Y.M.s & England to collect
funds for it.[13] They are two of the best & handsomest men
in Ohio Y. Meeting. The Committee lasted till 7 o'clk &
then we met as Ministers & Elders & sat till 10.30. Doctrines
were freely discussed & I was requested to speak at some
length, which I did. I trust I did not injure the cause, but
the old view of Barclay "Vehiculum Dei" was handed over
to me to explain or refute.[14] This I was helped to do to

[13] John Butler (1803–1887) was born in New Jersey, but spent most of his
life in Ohio. He was active in many reforms, participated in an interview with
President Abraham Lincoln in 1862, and attended the Richmond Conference
in 1887. H-DQB.
[14] This had to do with the controversy over the "Inner Light" and W.R.'s

general satisfaction, but it was a time of mental strain &
religious exercise.

3rd day 28th Meeting of Ministers & Elders at 8 o'clk,
a very interesting time, much counsel & sound doctrine.
The queries read & answered: I omitted to mention (I
believe) in its proper place last week, the reading of our
English General Epistle but for some reason D. Updegraph
objected to give, he protested it should not be printed &
circulated, as has been always the case, & he seems always
able to settle a point. The Yearly Meeting was a united
one to day of men & women. Edith Griffith's testimony
was read & great deal preached about her.[15] Then a young
friend gave us some extremely interesting particulars of
his work in Tennasee with Dr. Gardner.[16] He says, less
than half the White population there, can read or write.
The coloured people are educated in connection with Fiske
University & the Jubilee singers, but the poor Whites are
fearfully degraded. D. Updegraph rose, & said, "let us,
right on the spot, raise them 400 dollars. All who will
give 10 dollars stand up," 22 did so "Now who will give
5 dollars"—their names were all put down by the clerk
& then hats handed round for single dollars & the required
sum was raised! Well done Ohio Y. Meeting. Then the
Mission report was read. Over 1000 mission meetings have
been held during the year & 70 people converted. No

expression indicates he did not fully accept Robert Barclay's beliefs. Barclay
said in part," . . . *but we understand a spiritual, heavenly, and invisible principle, in which God, as Father, Son, and Spirit dwells;* a measure of which
divine and glorious life is *in all men* as a *seed,* which of its own nature draws,
invites, and inclines to God; and this some call *vehiculum Dei,* or the *spiritual
body of Christ,* . . ." *Apology* (New York, 1832), pp. 137, 138.

[15] Edith (Price) Griffith (1801–1873) had twice visited in the British Isles
and also traveled in the ministry in many American yearly meetings. There is
no explanation available for the gap between her death and the approval of
this memorial minute. *Memorial, Edith Griffith* (New Vienna, Ohio, n.d.;
London, 1878). H-DQB.

[16] He means Dr. J. D. Garner (1831–1917), who founded the Maryville
Normal and Preparatory School for white children in Tennessee. Warner,
Yardley Warner, p. 15.

Friend is in the drink trade. Only two friends use strong drink & the report adds, "Over 200 use tobacco, but these are only recent conversions & they have not yet learned that smoke is part of the filthiness they have to lay aside as Christians." After meeting A. Kimber & I borrowed a Buggie of mine host & drove about 2 or 3 miles to K. & C. Talbots. It *was* sweet to be under their roof. They have a comfortable little home very like Australian, but is unfinished, not plaistered inside, either walls or ceilings, in some rooms. Dear C. T. just as nice and loving as ever. Kinsey took me round his homestead which is nice. They farm 70 acres, have a vineyard & a large peach orchard not quite come into bearing yet. The heat today is almost terrible in the sun & 100 in the shade. At the meeting-house, Friends have a tin bucket & tin ladle & we help ourselves as we want. Everything is in homely style. In the evening we had the concluding meeting of Ministers & Elders, a very favored time, much plain speaking in love. Did not break up till nearly 10:30.

4th day 29th After our early breakfast which is followed by reading & usually 5 or 6 prayers, G. K. Jenkins drove J. N. Richardson & me in his carriage to see the ruins of the boardingschool. It has a remarkable history. After the separation 20 years ago of the Wilburite party in Ohio—the school remaining 14 years in the hands of the Wilburite party—a lawsuit was commenced & settled in favour of the sound Friends. The Yearly Meeting set to work & repaired it thoroughly, & just as it was finished but the school had not assembled in it, it was set on fire & burnt down. Foul play on behalf of some of the Wilbur Friends is strongly suspected, but of course nothing was proved. It is in a lovely spot & I do hope somehow the money will be raised to rebuild it. Then went to the devotional meeting where a young girl (Carrie somebody) confessed that Christ was not only *the* great Physician but her *whole* Physician, for he had healed her body & limbs of an incurable malady, after her conversion. She gave the most thrilling details. Then the great midweek meeting for worship was held & was a memorable time. Esther Slade & W. Robson had the principal preaching, but several others followed, all in harmony such as I never saw exceeded. My address was under a solemn feeling that it would be my last to Ohio Y. Meeting which closes tomorrow. S. Satterthwaite & William Allen (the black minister —born a slave) offered prayer & my dear wife & children were prayed for. Went to dine at Jonathan Binns. His name is well known in England as for many years clerk of the sound body.[17] He is feeble but very full of love. Met a large company of Friends there & had much sweet converse. My kind friend Anthony Kimber left me to return to his home this afternoon, his wife's health making his longer absence undesirable. He is a choice man, a thorough liberal, in a meeting of such rank conservatives, as we know little of in England—I mean Philadelphia Friends. A Kimber's brother W. B. Kimber we have a little book about, at home.[18] His brother Thomas is a great revival preacher & poet. The Yearly Meeting met again in joint session this afternoon. Many reports were passed—a long spirited discussion on the peace question. The war here has left its marks as to peace views, among some Friends.

I want my dear friends to see the glorious great Butterflies about here, also the tiney Hummingbirds flitting from leaf to leaf but never apparently settling. Shumack trees are very abundant, both Stagshorn & the bearded, but I do not see great difference in the foliage between ours at home & this. The old burnt tree stumps are verily

[17] Jonathan Binns (b.?–1883) was clerk of Ohio Yearly Meeting at the time of the Wilburite-Gurneyite separation in 1854. H-DQB.
[18] *Memoir of William B. Kimber* (Philadelphia and London, 1852), who died at the age of thirteen in 1849.

Australian so are the Snake fences & square planned streets, not all made yet. Some of the side streets of Mount Pleasant remind me exceedingly of the cross streets between Crown & Smith Street Wollongong. I intend to post these two sheets to night & the reply if sent off within a day or two of receiving this, should be sent to care of John F. Morgan as last.

5th day 8th Mo: 30th Went to the devotional meeting at 8 o'clk—a wonderful time! I believe everyone there (some 200) all said something. I give from memory a very few. "I rejoice in the Lord." "The Lord saves me just now." "I am trusting in the blood." "I wish to say I used to judge everybody, but Jesus has taken all the judge out of me." "I have not been so happy in the Lord as I desired, but I wanted Him to work in my way." "Ah brother! thee will never fix it so anyhow." "I am happy in Jesus." "Bless the lad! he was only converted last night." A rank Hicksite & a Wilburite were converted at about 11 o'clk last night. I see & feel it *is* the Lord's work & it is marvellous in my eyes. Old Friends of 80 in the straight-coats & bonnets rise, with the tears pouring down their cheeks, to say, how happy they are in the love of Jesus & how He has delivered & saved them. The last sitting of the Y. Meeting began about 10 o'clk & lasted without intermission till 5 o'clk in the afternoon. John Butler said, he felt a religious concern that *our* Yearly Meetings Epistle, after all, should be reprinted & published & after a long discussion it was fixed to be so. Dear S. Satterthwaite & C. Talbot came into our meeting & the former spoke & C. T. prayed. They have a curious way here. There are two women Friends appointed as "messengers" to the Men's meeting & they suddenly appear & walk arm in arm, up to the clerk's desk, without knocking or any intimation of their presence. When any subject is before the meeting for discussion, it is generally settled thus, "Now then, who wishes this to be done?" "I do," "so do I," " thats my feeling." I feel comfortable." "I like that." "that is so, &c" I do not see why this plan is not as good as our London plan, & much quicker. I am furnished with a very full returning Certificate. Ten Epistles were passed & a great deal of routine business & then prayers were offered. I felt constrained to pray for the separated body as well as the sound Friends. Thus closed Ohio Y. Meeting for 1877 "to be held at Damascus next year, if the Lord will." It has been a very blessed time. It seems singular that the old meeting house here, should be used by three Yearly Meetings. The Wilburites hold their Y. Meeting next month & the Hicksites in the Spring. It is a queer plain old place & the floor would probably look cleaner, if they used spittoons, but that is only American! Had a late dinner at G. K. Jenkins & then a very sweet prayer meeting in his parlour—a company never expecting to meet again on earth! Retired early as we have to be off at 4.30 in the morning. Many Friends left this evening in vehicle for Portland Station.

III. On to Iowa Yearly Meeting

6th day 8 mo. 31st. Breakfasted at 4 o'clk & then we took leave of our dear friends the Jenkins family & about 150 friends were conveyed in all sorts & conditions of vehicles to Portland Station, over as bad a 7 miles of road as I ever wish to travel. J. N. Richardson parted from me at Stubinville he to continue his work in this Y. Meeting & New York, & then to return to his beautiful home at Lessue. I parted with dear S. Satterthwaite at Wellsville, she going on towards Philadelphia, I getting into a train for Cleveland. Had the company of C. Talbot on the journey. She is on a religious visit to her own Y. Meeting. Got to Cleveland at 1.35. It is one of the prettiest cities I ever saw—150,000 inhabitants, one street called Euclid Avenue is 6 miles long, houses all the way, both sides, I believe. The city is quite close to the seashore, alias the shore of Lake Erie, in all appearance sea, only fresh water. James & Meribah Farmer took C. Talbot & me to lodge in their beautiful house.[1] Scarcely had we got in, than a furious storm began—awful crashing thunder, hail & wind. One Friend, who travelled with me, was met with the news, his chimney had gone right through his house. He & his wife are named Alton & Theodate Pope. Trees lay prostrate in the street & we hear much serious harm has happened in this city. Drove in two Buggies (3 miles) through incessant lightening to the meetinghouse which we reached about 8 o'clk & met (I think) 26 Friends, but we had a precious time & I felt well repaid for coming to Cleveland. Retired at 10 o'clk. Poor old Brigham Young has gone to his account (on the 29th) leaving about 70 widows to

---

[1] James Farmer (1802?–1891) was an elder and president of a bank in Cleveland as well as president of the Cleveland and Pittsburgh Railroad. His wife Meribah was a minister. H–DQB.

mourn his loss. Would it were a death blow to Mormonism.

7th day 9th Mo: 1st Left Cleveland at 7 o'clk this morning, the train passing for several miles along the shores of Lake Erie, whose waves were dashing up against the breakwaters in grand style. It seemed impossible to think it is only a freshwater lake & not the ocean after all. Had the company of Richard Harkness, an Ohio minister, as far as Toledo, & thence I was unattended the rest of the long 13 hours railway journey of nearly 400 miles, from Cleveland to the great new city of Chicago. We came quite close to Lake Michigan for miles before approaching Chicago, & in the twilight saw a grand Prairie fire about 3 miles from the train. Joseph Jones met me at the Depot & took me in a horse car, to his pretty little house, no. 1083 Indiana Avenue, where his wife & daughters gave me a kind & hearty welcome. It is very refreshing in a land of strangers to meet any one who has been in England & better than all, Joseph Jones has seen my dearest wife. Chicago is a marvellous place of more than half a million inhabitants. There are still sad marks of the awful fire of 6 years ago, but it is wonderful how they have rebuilt the city. Whole blocks of ruins still remain, but for the most part splendid shops & buildings line the great wide streets, & tram Omnibus's run everywhere.

1st day 9th Mo: 2nd Went to meeting in a very nice carpeted meetinghouse & met there Stanley & Sarah Pumphrey & Susan Doyle & Helen Balkwill.[2] It was a great treat to see those who had left England a week after I did. After I had offered prayer, H.B. preached very sweetly, then I spoke at some length & Stanley closed in prayer. They all joined us at J. Jones's to dinner. At 5 o'clk, the P.s & I went to a meeting for worship held in town some

---

[2] Susan Doyle was a member of Carlow Monthly Meeting, of Dublin Yearly Meeting. Two years later she accompanied Sarah Satterthwaite on a journey to Norway.

3 miles from here & Stanley & I had much service there. Then hurried back to J. Jones's to tea & Helen B. & I went to a 7.30 meeting in the meetinghouse, in which we were both very largely engaged—I for nearly an hour & we were greatly blessed. I omitted to mention the school held in a room under the meetinghouse after morning meeting. There are classes for children & others for adults—all Friends, or connected with them. Everybody comes & learns, old & young, rich & poor, the most adapted for it, being the leader or teacher of the class. A day of special mercy!

2nd day 9th mo: 3rd After an early breakfast, Dr. Matthew Oliver Jones (brother of my host) called in his Buggie & took me a lovely drive for several miles along the Boulevards of Chicago, to Hyde Park. Surely this city is unprecedented in its rapid growth. It has only existed 40 years & was burnt down 6 years ago. It has half a million of inhabitants & is as full of grand buildings as if 100 years of prosperity had gone over it. I fear my friends at home will think I am talking large, like "brother Jonathan" has the character of doing, but he has something large to talk about at Chicago.[3] Went to J. Jones's office & with him to the Chamber of Commerce, where about three million dollars change owners every day. J. J. is a Produce Agent & sells by telegram to Liverpool, bacon, cheese &c. He just sold 3000 casks of bacon while I was by his side. There is one establishment 6 miles from here, where they kill 6000 pigs every day on the average, & salt them for export. They make about 6 cents (3d) per lb by the cask. Went to the noonday prayer meeting which is held every day & was very nice, then to see Farwell Hall where Moody has won so many souls for Christ, also to

[3] "Brother Jonathan" was another symbol of the United States, like "Uncle Sam."

the tabernacle where he preaches.[4] This is, as it were, his city. Dined with J. Jones in town & then went to a daily temperance meeting where many spoke of their own experience. Then J. J. took me a drive along the lake shore to the great waterworks. Chicago is supplied by water drawn from the Lake two miles from shore, in a tunnel under the Lake & the engines are considered the finest in the world—one is 1.400 horse power & the other 1000. This is a great city for fast trotting horses, driven with a long straight whip with no lash. J. J. drove me one mile in three minutes. We passed Mr. Pulman's the sleeping car inventor.[5] He has one of the best houses in Town. I visited an hotel making up 1000 beds. This is large talk, but indeed it is true. Made two calls & then the Pumphreys joined us to tea. Josiah Simms is a very active useful man here. He is a brother of Marshall Simms & nephew of our poor old friend. At 9 o'clk in the evening we left the Jones's & took our places in a Pulman Car where we five English friends each had a very comfortable bed & left Chicago at 10 o'clk & were (I believe) all soon asleep.

3rd day 9th mo: 4th Rose at about 6 o'clk in time to see us cross on a fine iron bridge the queenly river Mississippia, navigable 2000 miles, a splendid river such as I never saw before. Then stopped for breakfast & went on through Prairie land into Iowa state & then we began at the stations, to pick up Friends, till our cars were crowded. I was delighted to welcome dear Joel & Hannah Bean— just as full of love as ever they were—& find them full of questions about my Tenie & Mabel & parents & Priscie & the Gibsons &c.[6] Dear old Joseph Hoag elder brother of

---

[4] Dwight L. Moody (1837–1899) a famous interdenominational evangelist, who, with his song leader Ira D. Sankey (1840–1908) held revivals everywhere in this period. DAB.

[5] He refers to George M. Pullman (1831–1897) who had organized the Pullman Palace Car Co. a decade earlier. DAB.

[6] Mabel Grace Robson, eldest child of Walter and Christina Robson, born in 1871; George Stacey and Elizabeth Gibson, referred to earlier by initial at

L. M. Hoag, also came & sat by me awhile.[7] Reached
Oscaloosa at 1.30 & John H. Green met me & took me &
J. & H. Bean to be his guests during Y. Meeting. One great
disappointment which rather weighs me down, is the fact
of no home news since the letter from my dearest, posted
two days after I left. I thank God, that while I was writing
the last sentence, Sarah Green knocked at my door & said,
"if thee'll come down, I'll give thee a letter," & now I have
a sweet long letter from my dearest, dated up to the 23rd
ult. I must not give way to being anxious, but it is but
a poor account of my precious wife & not first rate of my
dear parents, but to have heard at all makes me overflow
with gratitude, for "hope deferred makes the heart sick."
Oscaloosa is a city of 6000 inhabitants & 20 miles of streets.
The paths are all made of wood planks. It is the capital
city of Mahaska county. After dinner, Charles Hutchinson
& wife called to see me. They only left England about
a week before I did. They live 4 miles out of town or I
should have stayed with them, but am very comfortable
here. There is a meetinghouse here, called the city meeting
with three Ministers & congregation of nearly 200 Friends,
& a mile away is the Yearly Meeting house, with a still
larger congregation chiefly of Friends living a little way
out of Oscaloosa & near Penn College a large fine building
for Friends sons & daughters. Called on two families with
the Beans & after tea went to the Representative Meeting,
(late Meeting for Sufferings) where was read a very long
testimony concerning Mary Pinkham deceased.[8] It took
over an hour to read.

---

the end of the entry for August 24. George Stacey Gibson (1818–1883) was
clerk of London Yearly Meeting at this time, was a banker, and supporter of
the British and Foreign Bible Society. L-DQB.

[7] Joseph Hoag (1801?–1880) and Lindley Murray Hoag (1808?–1880) were
both ministers and the sons of Joseph Hoag (1762–1846) another minister.
Lindley Murray Hoag made two visits to Europe, and was overwhelmed by
attention on his first visit. H-DQB.

[8] Mary (Beede) Pinkham (1802–1877) was a minister who was born in New

4th day 9th Mo: 5th Breakfasted early & walked with
Joel Bean to the meetinghouse (a full mile away) where,
at 8 o'clk was held Iowa Yearly Meeting of Ministers &
Elders. The following certificates for Ministers & their
companions were read. I cannot remember which Y.M.s
in America the American ones came from, viz Stanley &
Sarah Pumphrey, W. Robson, Helen Balkwill, David Mac-
Millan, Julia Ann Miles, Jesse Lloyd, Samira Trueblood
& her husband, Samuel Trueblood & his wife Priscilla,
Franklin Meridith, William Thornbury, Amos Bond,
Francis C. Stanley, Robert Knight & James Jackson.[9] Much
thankfulness was expressed for our presence. It was very
pleasant to meet dear old David Hunt, also John F. Hanson.
The latter has just lost his dear wife, leaving him with
eight children. Meeting for worship began at 10 o'clk. The
lower meetinghouse was very full. It seats 1000 (the upper
one is just like it in size & arrangement, one on the top of
the other). A dear old woman Friend, quite blind, offered
prayer & spoke, then Stanley P. spoke. I followed at considerable length, then a woman turned my concern into
a prayer, some shorter communications & I closed in prayer.
Home to dine & then began Iowa Y. Meeting. All the
certificates read again, which was very tedious & various
committees set apart. A very painful circumstance has
occurred. Bear Creek quarterly meeting has sent up two
lists of representatives, two sets of Answers to the queries
&c. The clerk, Joel Bean said we could receive neither

Hampshire, and lived later in Pennsylvania and Ohio before moving to Iowa.
She traveled widely in America, and made two journeys to the Pacific Coast
in her later years. "Memorial of Mary B. Pinkham," *Minutes of Iowa Yearly
Meeting*, 1877: pp. 31–34.

[9] The Minutes listed the following visiting ministers: Stanley and Sarah
Pumphrey, Walter Robson, Helen Balkwill (all of London); Amos Bond (Indi-
ana), Robert Knight (Indiana), Jesse Loyd (Ohio), David Macmillan (Western),
Julia Ann Miles (Indiana), Franklin Meredith (Western), Francis C. Stanley
(Ohio), William Thornberry (Indiana), Samira Trueblood (Western), Samuel
Trueblood (Western), and Rachel Woodard (Kansas). John Henry Douglas of
Indiana arrived late. The Minutes do not mention the James Jackson listed in
the Journal. *Minutes of Iowa Yearly Meeting*, 1877: p. 2.

till it was decided which was the right one & it was referred
to all the representatives. S. P. & I were invited to join
this body & we met in the evening. It soon became clear
that a body of over 200 members of Bear Creek Quarterly
Meeting have separated & set up a Quarterly Meeting of
their own, taking five recorded ministers with them. They
separate because they say, Friends have forsaken the old
paths, Barclay, &c. They are in short Wilburites. It was
finally decided to report to the Yearly Meeting which was
the proper list of representatives &c. and to advise the
appointing of a committee to visit the Quarterly Meeting,
to try & restore, in the spirit of meekness.

I would like my dear ones to see Iowa Yearly Meeting.
The house stands in a large plot of ground, where are
hundreds of horses & Buggies & waggons & groups of
Friends eating their meals on the grass, & white tilted vans
& tents where families of Friends are camping out, day &
night. I asked one Friend what his wife & self would do
if it rained in the night. He said if it was very bad they
would go into the meetinghouse. The dear people are
many of them too poor to be able to afford lodging at a
boarding house & being somewhat uncouth & many of
them Norwegians seem to prefer the independence of
camping out. There are lots of lovely babies in both Mens
& womens meetings, some in long clothes & some just short
coated. They touch my heart greatly.

5th day 9th Mo: 6th 1877. S. Pumphrey, H. Balkwill,
Susan Doyle & I went to the meetinghouse at 8 o'clk &
met in No. 2 committee room with the dear Friends of
Bearcreek Q. Meeting who have represented the separated
body & had a long open time with them. We begged them
not to complete the separation & spoke very lovingly &
earnestly & much prayer was offered. The poor dear Friends
took our labours very kindly & we feel we have done *our*
duty, but they replied *they* had not left us but we were

FIG. 2. Photograph of Iowa Friends camping across from the yearly meeting-house at Oskaloosa.

leaving them. *We* had left our first principles, thought lightly even of Barclay's Apology & as such the command had gone out, to them, to come out & be separate. Y. Meeting met at 10 o'clk & was opened by S. Pumphrey in prayer. The first subject was the Committee's report as to Bearcreek & then a committee was appointed to select suitable Friends to visit that Quarterly Meeting & to labour with the separated Friends, if possible. Passed sundry reports & at 12 adjourned for an hour's recess. It was a picturesque sight to see all Iowa Yearly Meeting probably 1500 Friends picknicing on the grass outside the meeting-house in groups, sitting on the soft grass, discussing peaches, grapes & more solid viands. I was asked "out" to lunch with some Friends, not my hosts party, under the trees with some other dear Friends. Some Friends feed *in* the meetinghouse. This is not so well, as it brings such hosts of flies which buzz about during the sittings, to our constant annoyance. Reassembled at 1 o'clk & read the answers to the Queries &c. I spoke on the fact that 600 families in Iowa do not read the Bible in their families, & spoke of the privilege of it & of family prayer. Dear David Hunt followed & said he always prays with his wife vocally, every day. Several other Friends followed in a similar strain & then we adjourned till tomorrow morning. Home to my quarters to a meat tea. Then met in a committee room, a committee of Friends to decide on a proposal from Indiana to form a Friends Foreign Mission association. S. P. & I plainly laid the case before them feeling that they hardly realized the pecuniary burden they were bringing on themselves. They have their own N. American Indians to labour with & they at last decided to do as Ohio has done, decline to join with Indiana. At 7 o'clk the great annual Temperance Meeting was held. Laurie Tatum in the chair.[10] S. P. H. B. & I, all spoke at some length, others followed & "Hold the Fort" was sung. Home to bed (rather weary), at 10 o'clk. I omitted to say, that when we had broken up the Y. M. this afternoon & were all in the yard outside, a Friend from Bear creek called out from a top window that they had hired the city Hall & invited all who sympathised with them, to meet with them there to hold a Y. M. Meeting, or to that effect, so I fear the separation is an accomplished fact, & they will draw away many disciples after them.

6th day. 9th Mo: 7th. The weather here, continues perfect for the Y. Meeting—the nights cool & Autumn like, the days warm & bright. Oscaloosa is a curious place, extending over so much ground that it certainly has no appearance

[10] Lawrie Tatum (1822–1900) was one of the early Quakers in Iowa, and took an important place in the Indian work of Friends. He was the author of *Our Red Brothers* . . . (Phila., 1899). See: Louis T. Jones, *The Quakers of Iowa* (Iowa City, 1914); *Minutes of Iowa Yearly Meeting,* 1901: pp. 71–73.

of being either a town or a city, but built & planned on the wide Prairie land. 1200 miles west of Philadelphia land is plentiful & the houses stand on their own ground. There is one square where are good Stores & much business is done.

On reaching the meeting of Ministers & Elders at 8 o'clk this morning, my heart was gladdened by welcoming dear J. H. Douglas, come with certificate, for service in this & Ohio Y. Meetings. He & I had much service very solemnly both in that meeting & in the Y. Meeting afterwards on the state of the Society. After lunch again on the grass I took H. B. & her companion to visit the dear Friends living in their tents & waggons, who seemed pleased to see us & shake us by the hand. They struck us as wonderfully like gipsies at home, but when they come into the meeting house, the women don very large Friends Bonnets & look very proper. There are a great many Norwegian Friends here, who give us a very warm welcome.[11] Had a long & very stirring conference on Mission work after the recess. I glean a few particulars of facts concerning Iowa Y. Meeting, brought out by Answers to the queries. There are 8846 members included 182 separated just now —increase this year 256. 29 sell tobacco, 9 cultivate it, 557 males use tobacco & 102 females!! After tea, went to a very interesting committee on the work among the North American Indians & then to a very large meeting, called at the request of Robert Knight for all the preachers. He, S. P. & I had large service in it, & I believe God was glorified.

7th day 9th mo: 8th. Went to the devotional meeting at 8 o'clk—a solemn favored time, not so excited as those in Ohio. One man's experience was strange. He said, "I

---

[11] The first Norwegian Friends arrived in 1840, and others followed. The meeting at Stavanger, named for their Norwegian Quaker center, was recognized in 1864. Lindley Murray Hoag was one of the ministers who had visited among Friends in Norway. Jones, *The Quakers in Iowa*, pp. 175–180.

only know two sorts of people converted & unconverted
& the former rejoice in Christ Jesus & have no confidence
in the flesh." "Well brother is that thy experience"? "I
worship God. I don't worship ministers." As soon as the
Y. Meeting met, I asked leave to visit the women's meeting
& was most heartily liberated. David McMillan & Samuel
Trueblood having like concerns, went with me. I had a
great deal to say & my brethren not very much, but we
were there nearly two hours. The sisters expressed (far
too warmly) their satisfaction with my visit. Lunched on
the grass & then came into the 1st day school conference
which S. P. H. B. & I all spoke at, but I gave way for
J. H. D. feeling he was the man that ought to speak, &
so he did, splendidly. I went to tea at Cyrus Beedes &
met several Friends there, C. Hutchinson & his wife among
the number.[12]

1st day 9th mo: 9th. The weather (heretofore so fine &
bright) has changed & today is a steady downpour of
rain making the streets of Oscaloosa (which are only sand)
one mass of black mud. The wooden footpaths are just
indispensable a day like this. Thousands of persons were
expected by cheap trains to day, to be at the meetinghouse,
& Friends here seem thankful it is wet, for they say the
trains, when it is fine, bring a surging mass of pleasure
seekers, who block up the meetinghouses, go in & out, now
listening to one preacher & then to another, some preaching
in the open air. Today, there have just been enough to
fill both houses. Went to the devotional meeting at 8 A.M.
& then S. P. & I decided to be together upstairs, leaving
J. H. Douglas the lower meeting. We had a good meeting
in which after S. P. had prayed I spoke for nearly an hour
& several followed in perfect union. Friends had brought

[12] Cyrus Beede (1828–1908) was born in New Hampshire and after teaching
in various places moved to Iowa in the 1850's. He worked for Indians for forty
years, and was one of the founders of the publication, *Western Work*. H-DQB.

their dinners & so hundreds of us, in different parties dined in the two meetinghouses & at 2 o'clk began the afternoon meetings. S. P. & I again were announced for upstairs, & we had nearly all the service. It was a very solemn meeting & many tears were shed. Home to tea at my quarters, J. H. Douglas with me, & after tea had an intensely interesting conversation with him on the doctrine so constantly & almost exclusively preached here & at Ohio —complete sanctification. Joel Bean & J. H. D. do not see alike on it, differing in love. At 7.30 John Green took me to the congregational chapel where I had been announced to preach tonight. I spoke for about an hour, the minister having gone through the preliminaries. Called at the Friends city meetinghouse on my way home & heard dear Hannah Bean very sweetly, also two other ministers. Home to bed.

2nd day 9th Mo: 10th 1877. The rain has given place to most beautifully fine weather today, but the roads are entirely impassable for foot passengers & the Buggies are sinking in nearly to the Springs. The wooden paths are really invaluable. Meeting of Ministers & Elders at 8 o'clk, much counsel given on various subjects. Meeting at 10 o'clk—Routine business. After lunch on the grass, assembled men & women in joint conference to hear the Memoir of Mary Pinkham. Then Penn college was taken up & a collection introduced "in the very face of the meeting," similar to what I described in Ohio, Laurie Tatum being in this case, the leader. $1000 were raised towards completing the building. After meeting, Samuel Neave (late of Fordingbridge) son of the late M. A. Neave drove me & Elizth. Hutchinson 4 miles to Charles Hutchinson's pretty home. S. N. lives with the Hutchinson's. Greatly enjoyed an evening of religious intercourse with these devoted Christian people. Their foreman, living near them & another man joined us at evening reading. Lodged there.

It is a sweet home in the country, far away from folk. They have 4 sons fine good lads & one daughter, Mabel, about 10 years old, I think.

3rd day 9th Mo: 11th. [includes 4th day] The boys took me to see two tame Coons kept in an outhouse. They abound here—curious creatures with 'possum like hair, bushy tails very beautifully striped. They are about as big as a Wallaby. Drove in to meeting at 9 o'clk. Surprised to find a woman Friend sitting near the Clerk, but her husband soon rose & said, his wife had been unjustly disowned by their Monthly Meeting & he was here to defend her rights. Joel Bean begged him to be quiet & said it could not be allowed, but as he remained speaking at the top of his voice, he was handed over to the doorkeepers or "caretakers," as they are called, who carried him out bodily; his wife followed on foot.[13] Then passed various reports & we had very fully expressed returning minutes given us. Then all the Epistles were passed and S. P. & I gave parting addresses. So ended Iowa Y. Meeting for 1877, after loving words from David Hunt & prayer from another Friend. I omitted to record a short visit from an American "sister" yesterday, to our meeting, very impressive and concise, only ¼ of an hour. Visited Penn College, the Professor showing us over it. It wants £ 3000 to finish & get it out of debt. This Y. Meeting closed under a blessed sense of the Lord's goodness to us all. His life-giving presence has been greatly felt in the meetings both for worship and discipline. The Pumphreys joined me at dinner at J. H. Green's and afterwards we explored the city of Oskaloosa, visiting some of the great business stores &c. Called to see H. Balkwill & her companion & took leave of them, not expecting to meet again till they return to England in 2 years, or more. They intend going to Kansas in a few days. Took tea at Henry Spencer's, where the

[13] The official Minutes of the yearly meeting ignored this episode.

Pumphreys make their home. Then back to my quarters & packed up & took (probably) the last leave in this world, of J. & H. Green & their family, Mabel, Clara & boy, whose name I forget. Mary Tyrrell (H. Green's mother) a very dear old friend, lives with them. She is sister to G. K. Jenkins of Mount Pleasant, Ohio. The P's & I met at the Depot & as there was no sleeping Car we took our seats in a chair Car—J. F. Hanson also with us. Left Oskaloosa at 9.30. The attendant let back the backs of our lounging chairs so as to make us sort of couches of them, & we got snatches of sleep during the night. Just at sunrise, we were at the town of Keokuk & crossed the great river Mississippi on a fine iron bridge there. Travelled all day, only stopping once for a meal, & reached the city of Indianapolis about 6.30 in the evening. Our journey lay principally through country as flat as Cambridgeshire, once prairie, but now growing huge crops of Sargum & Maize, the latter selling here, at 5d per bushel. At Ottumwa (a place we passed) is a drink saloon with a big lamp on which are the words, "The way to Hell." The man who keeps it, protests to his customers that they are ruining themselves & if anyone calls for a glass of the best drink he sells, he gives them pure water. A curious mass of inconsistency! At Indianapolis, the capital of Indiana, a city of 100,000 inhabitants we were met by Friends who told us we could not get on to Plainfield till tomorrow & kindly offered us the needed hospitality for the night. William Pyles took me off to his very comfortable home, where after supper & hymns, I thankfully retired to bed, weary & dusty.

5th day 9th mo: 13th. It seemed an *accident* that we could not reach Plainfield last night, but I do not feel it so. Our dear friend, Rufus King's mother, had come here a few weeks back for medical treatment & died on 2nd day. The funeral to be at 9 o'clk this morning. I at once felt, I must be at it. I knew dear Rufus would like it, if he knew. Breakfasted at 7 o'clk & at 8. W. Pyles drove his wife & me to the house of R. King's sister, where the dear one died. Here we found a meeting of perhaps 30 Friends, sitting round the coffin. Three brothers & one sister of Rufus, being present. After a few verses from John 14, I prayed for them all & for dear Rufus. I remember how he used to speak of his precious mother who was a dear saintly woman. I then spoke & J. H. Douglas followed. Robert Knight sang a hymn & then John F. Hansen spoke most touchingly of the great loss he has sustained in the death of his wife. R. Knight offered prayer & then we were all invited to look at the face of the dead. The coffin was of polished rosewood & plated handles & gaudily handsome, with a large wreath & cross of white flowers on it. In the lid a large pane of plate glass, so that the body from the face to the breast was visible, most beautifully dressed in a sort of lace veil like a brides. It is an American custom. We then left the room while the weeping relatives took their last leave. Then J. H. Douglas & five other Friends carried the coffin to an open hearse with rich gold fringes & tassels, plate glass sides & doors. We all followed to the cemetry in buggies & here the coffin was placed on a shelf in a vault, to remain there till Rufus returns & decides where it shall finally rest. The mourners went in & J. H. D. offered a short prayer & the service was over. I afterwards went into the vault & saw numbers of boxes piled up, each containing a coffin waiting for final sepulture. It protects from the very prevalent habit here of body snatching. One face I looked at was a lady who had been deposited there 27 years, in nearly perfect condition.

IV. Western Yearly Meeting

(9th mo.: 13 cont.) To my quarters to an early dinner
& then to the Depot whence with about 200 other Friends,
we took the cars to Plainfield, 10 miles, where is held
Western Yearly Meeting. Met dear Robert Walter Douglas
in the train. I am very comfortably quartered at Elias
Johnson's—not Friends but very kind. With me are Barnabas & Rebecca Hobbs, powerful ministers (at least he is.)
Here I got a long letter from my precious wife, making my
heart overflow with thankfulness—a good account & it
tells of my Tenie having her own dear sister with her. This
I have longed to hear. At 3 P.M. went to the meeting on
Ministry & Oversight which I opened in prayer. Several
short addresses & then the Representatives were called
over & our various certificates read. Many American ones
as well as our English documents. J. & I. Jones of Chicago
met me very warmly. This is their own Y. Meeting. Several
who I met at Ohio were also very cordial—Wilson Spray
& wife & Elizth. Mallinson of New York.[1] Home to my
quarters to tea & then to a meeting for Worship in which
I had large service. Sarah Pumphrey & E. Mallinson also
spoke & then, after a hymn, the two "sons of thunder,"
the brothers Douglas spoke very powerfully. In the meeting on Ministry & Oversight Barnabas Hobbs was very
fully liberated to visit England, Ireland & the Continent [.]
I never heard so full an expression of unity. He is a fine
grey haired man of 60. I met also Dougan Clark's brother.
Wrote this & retired, somewhat weary, to bed.

6th day 9th Mo: 14 Devotional Meeting at 8 o'clk.
Certificates or Minutes for Friends of other Y. Meetings

---

[1] Wilson Spray (1833?–1886) was a minister who traveled among Friends,
and later accompanied W. R. to Kansas Yearly Meeting. *Friends Review* **39**
(1886): p. 681.

were read as follows, W. Robson & Sarah Pumphrey (Stanley's was last year) from England, E. Mallinson from New York, Daniel Hill, J. H. Douglas, Robert W. Douglas & Eliza Hodson from Indiana & Luther B. Gordon & John F. Hansen from Iowa.[2] A separation has taken place here as at Iowa & two sets of Representatives & Answers &c. came up from Plainfield Quarterly Meeting & sad to say, the separated ones are those who have long sat head of the meeting, the Bevan Braithwaite & Josiah Forster of Western Y. Meeting, men who have borne the burden & heat of the day.[3] As in Iowa, the decision of which representatives to receive, was handed over to the meeting of Representatives, answering to our large Committee in London.[4] Adjourned at 12 & came to my quarters to dinner. Meeting for Worship at 2 o'clk, from 1500 to 2000 present. Stanley prayed & then I spoke for a long while, followed by Stanley & Daniel Hill, all in perfect harmony, prayer from Robert Knight closed the meeting.[5] I think two solos were sung. Robert Douglas came with me to tea & converse about Australia. Then to the evening devotional meeting where Stanley read, prayed & spoke

[2] The Minutes also listed Robert Knight of Indiana, who had been at Iowa Yearly Meeting, and James E. Bailey of Iowa, who arrived late. *Minutes of Western Yearly Meeting of Men and Women Friends*, 1877, pp. 7, 66. Dougan Clark (1828–1896) was one of the leading evangelical ministers of the period. He studied at Haverford, and later prepared to practice medicine. Twice he was on the faculty of Earlham, and in 1877 he was visiting in the British Isles. He was one of the Friends who accepted water baptism in Ohio Yearly Meeting. H-DQB.

[3] Reference is to J. Bevan Braithwaite, who was for long years the principal author of the epistles of London Yearly Meeting, a Friend who visited America many times, and frequently entertained American ministers in his home; Josiah Forster (1782–1870), who was clerk of London Yearly Meeting for more than a decade, and served for half a century on the committee to correspond with Friends abroad. He made two journeys to America, and is a brother of William Forster (1784–1854) who was buried at Friendsville, Tennessee. L-DQB.

[4] While at an earlier date the Large Committee of London Yearly Meeting had been a body similar to the Representatives, since 1861 the Large Committee had been limited to preparing epistles for the consideration of the yearly meeting.

[5] W. R. preached from the text, "As for God his way is perfect," and stressed salvation through Christ. *Christian Worker* 7 (1877): p. 611.

a little while. I spoke & E. Mallinson & dear John F. Hansen followed & J. H. Douglas also. The most solemn meeting I have yet been at in America principally to the undecided ones, present. Greatly helped this day to my Saviour's praise. As I came to my lodgings I heard a most fearful screaming in a nice house on the way as if a lady was being murdered. I never heard so fearful a calling on God. I did not know what to do, so hurried home & found it was all right. They are spiritualists & the lady was having a powerful communication from one. Surely such can only be from Satan! The Western Y. Meeting is very large, the attendance probably larger than in London considerably, both houses about full. They are side by side as at Colchester &c.[6] They have a very novel way here with representatives. Any who are absent & no reason given— Friends are appointed to visit them & let them know they will be called on next Y. Meeting to say what they mean by such ways. In this & Indiana Y.M.'s (both in the state of Indiana) are over 25,000 Friends—truly a powerful army!

7th day 9th mo: 15th I conducted the devotional meeting, this morning, a very solemn favored time. I took for the leading idea of the meeting the transfiguration & the words, "Jesus only" with themselves. Y. Meeting at 10 o'clk. The report of the Committee about the two reports from Plainfield Q. Meeting, deciding in favour of the liberal one, was read & a very painful touching scene followed. Robert Hodson, a dear old Friend, rose & said, "he felt he & his party had no longer any rights or privileges among us," & he invited all, young & old who desired with him to maintain Friends principles in their purity, to withdraw to another place, where they might form a Yearly Meeting.[7]

[6] Colchester Meeting was in W.R.'s home quarterly meeting of Essex (after 1881 Essex and Suffolk).

[7] Robert Hodson (1797?–1882) was an elder in the local meeting at Sugar Grove. He died in Kansas, where he was traveling among the Friends in the

Several earnest appeals were made that they would not separate & especially the Clerk—Barnabas Hobbs L.L.D (Dr. Hobbs he is generally called) gave a thrilling appeal, but it was of no use & 99 men were counted out of the house. Meanwhile a very similar scene was enacted the other side of the shutters, in the Women's Y.M. It was *very very* sad. Had a long sitting, read London General Epistle & 6000 copies are ordered to be printed & circulated among their members. Read all the Epistles & sundry other routine & a committee is to be appointed to help this poor divided Q. Meeting. Adjourned at about 3 o'clk after sitting 2 hours & then 5 hours without intermission. After dinner was held at my request (S.P. also joining in it) a meeting for Ministers & all Christian workers. I began with prayer & then read Paul's address to the Ephesian elders; then S.P. spoke & I followed & then several Friends spoke in gratitude for the blessed time we had spent together.[8] Broke up at 6.20, hurried off to tea & at 7 o'clk was held the educational conference, addressed by Professor Pliney Chase from Philadelphia, a Friend, & considered one of the most learned men in America. His proofs of scripture & science being one, were beautiful & his argument of the reality of the "morning stars singing together," was I think, about the grandest thing we any of us, ever heard. S.P. & Dr. Hobbs &c. spoke briefly & broke up. The weather keeps very hot. I am in an almost constant

---

new Conservative yearly meeting established there in 1880. The *Friend* (Phila.) **55** (1882): p. 240. W. R., writing about this occasion many years later, reported that one of the visiting ministers from another yearly meeting, "sang at the top of his voice,

'See the mighty host advancing,
Satan leading on!'

When he had finished, he turned to me and said, 'I thought they should hear one more hymn before they went out.'" *British Friend*, N.S., **22** (1913): p. 288.

[8] The *Christian Worker* reported the English Friends imparted ". . . much plain, practical teaching on various points of special interest to those assembled." **7** (1877): p. 613. The *Friends Review* said, "the teaching was very much what was needed." **31** (1877): p. 123.

drip, day & night & am glad of the thinnest garments I possess, but it seems healthy weather, I think.

1st day 9th Mo: 16th A lovely warm bright morning & such a scene as I can never forget. Went to the morning devotional meeting, where the experiences & the prayers were unusually deep & striking. When this broke up, we went out while the shutters were removed & the great house all laid together. It was soon full & it seats 2,500— none standing. A rough stand, erected in the grounds out-side formed a centre for preaching to the throng in the yard. I was in the meetinghouse. S.P. opened in long earnest prayer, then I preached Christ & Him crucified with much liberty & power. Professor Chase followed me in a striking scientific appeal to the truths I had declared. S.P. followed beautifully, at some length, then a few shorter addresses, then J.H.D. very powerfully, & we broke up one of the largest, most solemn & quietest meetings I have ever seen. Meanwhile R.W.D., Amos Kenworthy & others preached to the throng out of doors.[9] As we left the ground, we noticed the little town of Plainfield looked like a country fair. People from Indianapolis & from all the country round, were here by thousands. Stalls for refreshments (all teetotal) were well supplied & patronized & the hotel at which the Jones's Pumphreys &c. stay, was so crowded with visitors, it was almost impossible to get food. It is judged there were over 10,000 people on the meetinghouse ground. Many only come for the spree of the thing, but I trust some "who come to scoff, remain to pray." At 2 o'clk, the great meetinghouse was again filled. I took up my place out of doors on the preaching stand & after "There is a fountain" had been sung, I spoke for half an hour to (probably) an audience of some 5000. Of

---

[9] Amos M. Kenworthy (1831–1917) was recorded as a minister in 1868, and often traveled among Friends. In 1893 he visited among Quakers in the British Isles. *Life and Works of Amos M. Kenworthy*. (Richmond, Ind., 1918). H-DQB.

course there were outsiders who would listen awhile, & then walk away & it is impossible to say how many of the vast crowd on the grounds really heard the words of Eternal life. R. W. Douglas followed me & then Robert Knight & for a few minutes Amos Kenworthy. "Shall we gather at the river" was sung & I closed in prayer. I never knew such an audience & all agreed they never saw one so quiet. Very many wept abundantly. After tea, of course thousands drove off in their Buggies & waggons which had lined the streets & camping ground, all day. S.P. addressed a little company in the Methodist chapel. I took my seat again in the great meetinghouse, there being only one meeting in the evening. I had a great deal to say & several followed, & now my voice is all gone for tonight, but it has been never better spent, I humbly believe. 1500 or 1600 were in the meetinghouse this evening, & now in looking back over this day & its great exercises & service, I do not know of one who spoke out of place, or out of the unity. In all the meetings the Gospel stream flowed freely, from repentance toward God, to fullest consecration to His service. I should say that the indoor meeting this afternoon was very satisfactory. J.H.D. spoke there an hour & half & S.P. spoke briefly I am told. To God, who had heard my earnest cry, to be helped this day, I would give all the praise, for the ability came only from Himself. A Baptist chapel between my lodgings & the meetinghouse has held the meeting today of the separated Y.M. & they have engaged that & the Presbyterian one, I hear, to hold their Mens & Women's Y. Meetings in, this week. I feel very tenderly for these dear friends who have become straightened in themselves. Now I must close this portion of my journal, to post in the morning. . . . This leaves me well in health & cheered on my way by renewed evidences granted that I am in my right place. My dear love to all my beloved relatives & friends.

Western Yearly Meeting 2nd day 9th Mo: 17th I could hardly believe till I had ascertained it from several to be true, that there were no less [than] 3000 carriages here yesterday, which reckoning an average of 4 to a carriage (many had 8. 7. or 6—some only 2 or 3) would make 12000 persons driven in from a distance besides all those, who like myself, are living or lodging in Plainfield. Meeting on Ministry & Oversight at 8 o'clk, Y.M. at 10 o'clk, a very interesting sitting on the state of the Society. The subject of paying Ministers was brought up & I spoke at some length, upon it & immediately almost, after I sat down in true American freedom Daniel Hill brought pencil & paper & requested me to write down as nearly as possible all I had said, or at any rate the headings, because he wanted to print it.[10] S.P. & J. F. Hansen spoke excellently. Closed at 2.30. I dined at the Hotel with the Jones's & many other Friends. Then back to meeting & at 4 o'clk to the Friends Foreign mission —very large. At the united request of many Friends I gave a sketch of my visit to the South Pacific Islands of which Friends in this land, seem to know nothing. I spoke for about 1¼ hours & was very warmly received.[11] After tea, a very interesting Home mission & 1st day school conference, Professor Chase & many others of us spoke & ere we parted we rose & sang, "What shall the harvest

[10] Daniel Hill (1817–1899) was editor of the *Christian Worker* and the *Messenger of Peace.* He had been in the state legislature, worked for peace and against slavery, and was recorded as a minister in 1863. He was Secretary of the Peace Association of Friends from 1869 until 1899. Indiana Yearly Meeting *Minutes,* 1900: pp. 193–196; *Christian Worker* **23** (1893): pp. 578, 579.

[11] He is quoted as having said, "Whatever we may think or say about the 'Inward Light' and its teaching to those who have never heard of revealed religion, one thing was manifest to him, the Bible and the missionaries have done more in a few years to lift these people up in the scale of social life, and a practical knowledge of the way of life and salvation through Jesus Christ, than the 'Inward Light' had done in all the ages that had passed." *Christian Worker* **7** (1877): p. 627. This quotation was read in England and led to a letter of protest to the *British Friend,* suggesting this was not a helpful thing to say, but assuming W. R. had been misquoted. **35** (1877): pp. 301, 302.

be," & I closed in prayer. So ended a day of much varied interest.

3rd day 9th Mo: 18th A heavy thunderstorm has at last, cooled the air so that there was a little frost in the night, & on going to the meeting on Ministry & Oversight this morning I found two great fires in each meetinghouse. The dear Friends here seem fearfully afraid of being cold. J.H.D. Dr. Hobbs & I had the principal service in the meeting on M. & O.—a meeting specially convened this time, not to transact business, but for religious exercise on the state of the Society. The Yearly Meeting met at 10 "in joint session" the shutters raised to hear & discuss many matters of mutual interest to men & women—a very interesting report of work among the South American Indians,[12] well spoken to, by several present who have laboured in that field & then a discussion on higher education & the necessity of having a Quaker college, if we will keep our young people as Friends, was earnestly advocated by Professor Chase, Dr. Hobbs & others. Adjourned at 3 o'clk, hurried home to dinner & met again at 4 to a Home mission meeting, which lasted till 6.15. Home to tea & met again at 7. for the Friends Bible Meeting. Professor Chase spoke for an hour & a half on the Bible—a speech I would like to have had printed. S.P. & I added a little. Meanwhile E. Mallinson & Sarah Pumphrey were holding a meeting with the young women. While we were in the yearly meeting this morning, letters were brought me in to the gallery from my dearest Tenie & Priscie. J.H.D. (who sits by me) said, if he was I, he would open them & so I did & read them through as a long report which I had heard before, was being read. Good accounts from home, cheer me inexpressibly & seem to come as answers to the prayers which I think I may truly say rise every hour that I am

[12] W. R. undoubtedly is referring to the work of Samuel A. Purdie (1843–1897) and others among the people of Mexico at Matamoros.

awake, for the health bodily, mental and spiritual of all my dear ones. It seems very kind of Professor Chase to be willing to attend this Y. Meeting. He is President of Haverford College, Philadelphia, but has been disowned by Philadelphia Friends for the sad crime of having in his drawingroom a pianoforte!! [13] At our meeting today, we had the company of Charles F. Coffin of Richmond. Some of my friends at home will remember his being at our Y. Meeting some time ago, with his wife. He gave me a very warm greeting, but left again in the afternoon to attend the funeral of his cousin, the celebrated Levi Coffin, one of the warmest friends to the poor slaves they ever had.[14] A very large funeral was expected. He died very suddenly while at his dinner on Firstday.

4th day 9th mo: 19th Meeting on Ministry & Oversight at 8 o'clk, a time of much interest & lively doctrinal discussion, lasting till about 11. Then meeting for worship. J. H. Douglas out of doors, most of the other ministers in the house. The principal vocal service was Stanley's & mine. I rejoice to say we labour side by side in greatest harmony. The meeting sat nearly 3 hours. After dinner a meeting on Anticapital punishment I did not attend, wishing to make a call, which I did on a dear old friend, a recorded minister, residing here for over 50 years, Eliezer Bales. He is now 83 years old, very loving & bright.[15] He traveled with my Grandmother 50 years ago & told me of his escorting her through the wilderness from here to Wabash & getting benighted, & all sleeping under a great tree. He is very patriarchal, his great grandchildren playing about the

---

[13] Actually, Thomas Chase, his brother, was president of Haverford College.

[14] Levi Coffin (1798–1877) died on September 16 at Avondale, near Cincinnati, Ohio. His *Reminiscences* are an important source about Quaker work for Negroes in this period. H-DQB.

[15] Eleazer Bales (1793–1887) was born in North Carolina, but moved to Indiana in the 1820's. He was recorded as a minister in 1829, traveled widely among Friends, labored for the Freedmen, and went to visit the new Conservative group in Kansas when ninety. H-DQB.

room. Poor dear old man, he has gone off now with the separatists, feeling no sympathy with the hymn singing &c. that has such constant place among Friends here. I do feel deep love & tender sympathy for him & his brother & sister separatists. I feel they have made a mistake to separate, but I also think there is on the part of many of the very earnest & active liberals, too great impatience of control & these dear old fathers feel they have no longer any influence over them. I paid the dear man such a visit as he said did he heart good, though of course in some things I differed from him. Then called on John Wood another separated friend but found him not so kindly disposed, though he received my visit very cordially & asked me to stay tea.[16] In the evening, went to the meetinghouse to hear lecture on the poor Indians delivered by Colonel Meachem—Colonel, not in the army but receiving that title from Government as Indian commissioner of peace! [17] He is a staunch friend of Red man & denounces in no measured terms the conduct of the United States government. He says, every Indian killed in war has cost the United States 10 white men & a million dollars (this is a positive fact). He was sent to try & prevent the late Modoc war, & on one occasion by the aide of General Kandy, saw the General shot dead, received 7 shots in his own body & was left for dead, but his life saved by Wi-ne-ma, an Indian woman, who knocked aside the rifles pointed at him. He is fearfully scarred, part of one hand shot off & the Indians had cut round his scalp & were commencing to raise it, when Wi-ne-ma again (I think) saved him. It was the most thrilling lecture I ever heard. The Government have given the Modoc tribe into the hands of the Friends of Western Yearly Meeting to take care of. Yearly

[16] John P. Wood (1805–1884) came originally from Maryland, but was active in the new yearly meeting at Plainfield. The *Friend* (Phila.) **57** (1884): p. 344.
[17] Colonel A. B. Meacham.

Meeting will, I suppose, close tomorrow. I have fixed to go with some Friends tomorrow evening to Monrovia, meeting there, next morning & one at Mooresville that evening, one at Easton the morning after, one at Beech Grove in the afternoon, on to Indianapolis & give a lecture there that evening & stay over 1st day in that city.

5th day 9th mo: 20th Closing meeting on Ministry & Oversight at 8 o'clk this morning. S.P. very earnest in prayer & afterwards very striking in ministry. He spoke of having heard some dear friends speak of the "Sin Principle" having been so completely eradicated from themselves that every root & fibre of it was destroyed, & he asked if they had really found it so. Several at once called out Yes! Yes! He spoke of its being a higher attainment than he had yet, or ever expected to attain. I followed him, on the two ideas now so prevalent, the one, the complete subjugation & the other, the destruction of the Sin Principle—how both seemed to yield the same fruit unto holiness & that there was abundant Scripture for the truth that as Christians, we were to "reckon ourselves to be *dead* indeed unto sin," but gave a loving caution as to expressing too much of one's own experience as to living without sin, in Public Meetings, because I believed that unconverted people would love to watch for our halting & that "he that says all that he knows, often says what he does not know." This was accepted, with much expression of unity. Closing sitting of Yearly Meeting was at 10. A great many reports to read & pass & all the Epistles to read. A very fully expressed returning Minute for me called out a sort of unity, carried by acclamation.[18] Near the close of the sitting, I offered prayer & praise. The closing minute was read at about 3 o'clk & Western Y. Meeting

---

[18] The Minute included the words, ". . . his solid deportment and sound gospel ministry have been truly edifying." *Minutes of Western Yearly Meeting* . . ., p. 65.

was over. Back to my quarters to dine & pack up. Took leave of many dear friends I have learnt to love & among the rest, Joseph & Isabella Jones, who, I expect never to see again. It is an odd sight in all these Y. Meetings, so many Friends (sometimes even women) bring into Meeting their long straight driving whips and sit with them stuck right up. J.J.R. knows the "American trotting whip" universally used in this land. Edmund Johnson & wife called for me, in their carriage & drove me along a real "bush road," through some "forest primeval" to their pretty home, at or near Monrovia some 13 miles from Plainfield. They are nice Friends with 3 grown up daughters & one small son. Spent the evening round a log fire in an open chimney on "Dogs," talking on religious experience almost entirely.[19] I almost dread the meeting which has been appointed tomorrow for me because the incubus in power here, belong to the party which have separated, but He who has ever helped me, will do so tomorrow, I have no doubt.

6th day 21st After breakfast, E. Johnson took me round his farm, where the great halfburnt tree stumps were wonderfully like Illawarra, indeed his whole home reminded me of it. Drove to meeting. Another friend, Scott was also there with a Minute & we both [had] much vocal service. I had some plain words to speak & to make the appeal to some, which they really loved best—the principles of the Society of Friends of Christ Jesus their Lord? I felt I had done what I could & left without the weight of a feather on my conscience. Took leave of Edwin & Asenath Johnson & her father (Lot Hadley) drove me home to his house to dinner. He is a fine elderly man with a youngish wife, both very nice. Went a lovely ramble in the bush after dinner. At 6.30. Lot & his wife & little son drove with me into Mooresville where I held a Public meeting, large & solemn, but I felt as if there were some

[19] "Dogs," or andirons.

very difficult to reach & I just had to keep on speaking for more than an hour before I could feel that I had delivered all the Lord had given me for them. John Taylor kindly took me in to lodge at his house.[20] He was one of the assistant clerks of the Western Yearly Meeting. I am now in the land of the great Sugar Maple trees from each of which on the average the settlers get 1 gal Molasses a year. They are very fine, tall, graceful trees.

7th day 9th mo: 22nd After breakfast, a young lad (whose name I forget) drove me 8 miles to Easton a little village of perhaps 500 people, where a meeting had been appointed for me, at 10 o'clk. About 200 (principally Friends) attended. Rachel Woodward prayed & after I had spoken, she & Mrs. Done spoke. Amos Mills drove me to his house to dine—Amos Done & his wife joining me there & we all drove to a meeting appointed for me at Decatur township, called Beechgrove meeting. This was crowded with Friends & others, & was a blessed time, closed by Amos Done in prayer, especially for my dear wife & children. John Millhouse drove me to his house to tea, & then his brother joined & drove us to Indianapolis to the meeting-house which was well filled & after Calvin Pritchard had read & prayed, I gave them my lecture on the South sea Islands, which was listened to with extreme attention.[21] My kind friend & host when at Indianapolis before, has made me welcome to his home again. William Pyle—& here I hope to stay till 2nd day.

1st day 9th Mo: 23rd Breakfasted at 7 o'clk, went to the Friends Bible School, very nice & instructive, then upstairs to the meetinghouse where many were gathered

---

[20] John A. Taylor (1841?–1881), about the same age as W. R., died not long after at the age of forty.
[21] Calvin W. Pritchard (1834–1896) was born and educated in Indiana, and lived most of his life there. However, it was at Wilmington, Ohio, in 1870 that his gift in the ministry was recognized. A powerful evangelist, he became editor of the *Christian Worker* in 1883, and held that position for nearly a decade. *American Friend* 3 (1896): pp. 1121–1123. H-DQB.

together, more than 300 I suppose, mostly but not all Friends. Dear E. Mallinson from N. York there & by me in the gallery. This was the 1st time, I think, I have seen beautiful bunches of exquisitely fragrant flowers in handsome vases on the gallery rail. After I had offered prayer, E.M. read John 17th & I spoke a long while, followed by E.M., then broke up. I found Lula Allen, a young lady passenger from Liverpool in the Pensylvania at meeting. I had promised to inform her if I came to Indianapolis & it was pleasant to see a face that I had first seen in the dear old country. She is daughter of a noted Dr. Allen & came out under the care of Dr. Harper. William Evans took me home to dinner with him & afterwards drove me 3 miles to the great Reformatory for female prisoners under the care of James & Sarah Smith, dear devoted Friends, the latter a recorded Minister.[22] All the female prisoners for long terms of years in Indiana, are sent here, also 130 girls, penitents, who had been vicious or were in danger of becoming so. They are sentenced to stay there till they reach the age of 18. & mostly turn out well afterwards. Indeed they are under such excellent training there, it would seem impossible it should be otherwise. E.M. joined me & we had a meeting with the women in a large upper room. On one side sat the prisoners 49 in number & 7 of them murderers (they do not hang in Indiana) sentenced for life. The other side, quite distinct, sat 130 girls the "Penitent class." A young man presided at a fine toned organ, like Sankey uses & they sang "I need thee every hour." also the young man sung solo "the ninety & nine." E.M. prayed. I read to them about Jesus in the house of Simon & the poor woman who was a sinner

[22] James Smith (1805–1885) and Sarah J. Smith (1814–1885) were both born in England, and came to America in 1845 after their marriage. Sarah J. Smith was the superintendent of the reformatory, and also a recorded minister. *Rhoda M. Coffin, Her Reminiscences*, p. 255, ff; *Friends Review* **38** (1885): p. 410; **39** (1886): p. 395. H-DQB.

washing His feet with her tears & wiping them with her
hair &c. &c. as I enlarged on His great love, the poor
creatures wept till I wept also. E.M. followed very beautifully, just simply telling her own experience. Then a
Christian lawyer who generally conducts service there,
asked if any wished to be prayed for & one poor prisoner
woman & one poor girl with streaming tears, rose, & we
had a blessed time. Many have been converted & one who
is a thorough Christian now, murdered a whole family.
She is there, for life & seems to have no wish to escape.
They could do so easily, as there are only two men on the
establishment & the gates we found wide open. Took tea
at Pleasant & Martha Bonds. They have two dear little
daughters about the ages of our precious little Mabel &
Ethel & they took to me nicely. Went to meeting in a
Mission Hall, Friends have hired, which was crowded,
owing to advertising an English Minister & had the best
time there, I have long known. I was weary & sleepy &
head-achey when we began, but I never felt more liberty
or power I think. Several lawyers, Ministers of other
bodies &c. were there. I look back on the last 3 days of
hard work, which I had dreaded, with peculiar thankfulness. It always feels painful to me to go to meeting
after meeting, where I am expected to preach & Friends &
others come to hear me, but God has been better to me than
all my fears, & I can lay me down tonight in peace & sleep,
commending my dearest wife, my sweet lambs & all my
loved ones to Him who loves us with a matchless love.

2nd day 9th mo: 24th The weather is only to be described as perfect, the sun hot & brilliant but the nights
cool & inclined to be frosty, so that one wakes in the morning refreshed with sleep After reading this morning, my
kind host W. L. Pyle offered earnest prayer for me & my
dearest ones & returned thanks for my visit. He is an elder
in the church, a very active Christian man. He is by trade

a dairy farmer—his farm several miles out of Indianapolis. He supplies the largest Hotels with their milk. I should judge him to be pretty comfortably circumstanced. He has an excellent wife, a grown up son in a wholesale Store in the city & 3 daughters of probably 18. 15. & 12 years. I post this before leaving by rail for Richmond this after-noon. The great Y. Meeting begins there tomorrow & I shall not get much time for writing. I am to be a guest of Charles & Rhoda Coffin as are also the Pumphreys (who spent yesterday there) & J. H. Douglas. Indiana is still the largest Y. Meeting in the world tho' there have already been three great offshoots from it—Kansas, Iowa & West-ern. They are planning another division I hear, but it is left at present. I enclose some cuttings from the India-napolis paper of this morning which will give my dear ones rather more particulars of myself, than I was aware of, before. I am thankful to report myself well in health.

V. Indiana Yearly Meeting

9th Mo: 24th 2nd day. Indianapolis. My kind friend W. Pyle drove me in his Buggie to the new cemetery, a very lovely spot, on the top & sides of a deeply wooded hill. In one place lie close together, several hundred soldiers killed in the civil war, each one's name marked on a small marble headstone. Calvin Pritchard called after dinner & then W.P. drove me to the Union Depot (Railway Station) calling on the way to inspect the new courthouse which is as grand & gorgeous as a million dollars & gilding & marble can make it. Took the cars (80 miles about) to Richmond, met at the station by Elijah Coffin. He drove me to his father's house, where a very loving welcome awaited me from dear Charles & Rhoda Coffin. Ushered into their two drawing rooms, I was introduced to their sons & their sons wives, also to a dear aged minister from Cincinnati Harriet Steer.[1] J. H. Douglas & the Pumphreys also make their home here for Yearly Meeting. A lovely home it is! C. F. Coffin & sons are bankers, men of great wealth & influence, C. & R. Coffin ministers of high standing in this land. My beloved Father will like to know that a card was read to me by R.C. from her aunt Mrs. Arnott with a message of warm love for the Yearly Meeting from her dear aged husband, Thomas Arnott. He is quite confined at home now, he is 87 years old, very bright, his memory unfailing, & what is better, has fully kept up with the times in his religious feelings as to sanctification, &c. Later in the evening arrived from Baltimore, James C. Thomas & his wife Mary Whitall. She is a sister

[1] Harriet (Harlan) Steer (1795–1883) was born in Pennsylvania, and after her family migrated to Ohio, she met Samuel Steer at Mount Pleasant and married him. While not born a Quaker, she joined in her youth. *Memory Sketches of Harriet Steer* (Concord, N.H., 1887); *Friends Review* **37** (1883): p. 106. H-DQB.

of H. W. Smith.[2] Thus I am in good company here, intelectually & spiritually. A good deal tossed & tried by receiving a note from the shipping Agents at Philadelphia, to say they have not a good vessel sailing on Nov. 15 & offer Dr. Hobbs & self two berths either on the 8th or the 22nd. If I leave on the 8th I shall leave my work undone, but to stay another week later is a great trouble to me. My poor dear wife I know wants me. Christmas business requires me at home & I seem not to know just what to do. Of course, Friends all say, stay another week.

3rd 9th mo: 25th Much deeply interesting converse with Dr. Thomas after breakfast. Meeting at 10 o'clk of Ministers & Elders. They are erecting a new Y. Meetinghouse in Richmond, which is to be ready next year. The old one is a poor shabby place, but seats a great many people. It is close to the Railway Depot which renders the situation very noisy & very dangerous, as the crossing is on the level—no gate & only the ringing of the bell on the engine to warn one of the near approach of the train. Several prayers & a short sermon from Stanley, then the following Minutes were read: W.R. & Sarah P. from England Deborah C. Thomas, James C. Thomas & Mary W. Thomas from Baltimore, Sarah E. Mallinson from N. York James E. Bailey & John F. Hansen from Iowa, Mary S. Elliot Joseph Blackledge, Isaac & Phebe G. Thomas from Ohio. The two latter are companions to E. Mallinson.[3] After a deal of welcome had been expressed, the clerk (Timothy Nicholson) asked for R. W. Douglas's concern & very sweetly & simply did the dear man spread his prospect for Australia, Tasmania & New Zealand before

---

[2] James Carey Thomas (1833–1897) and Mary (Whitall) Thomas (1836–1888) were active in many concerns in Baltimore. James C. Thomas was a physician, and the step-son of Deborah Thomas (*q.v.*) *Richard H. Thomas; Friends Review* **41** (1888): p. 811. H-DQB.

[3] David B. Updegraff arrived late, from Ohio Yearly Meeting. *Minutes of Indiana Yearly Meeting of Friends*, 1877: p. 96.

the meeting. He spoke of being at my house, talking to us about Australia & how that conversation (my Tenie will remember it) settled the concern in his mind.[4] I never saw so full an expression of unity. I think every one spoke— men & women. I prayed for him & his poor dear invalid wife & his aged mother & afterwards gave a short sketch of the kind of work before him. After this was over, an elderly Friend (Levi Jessup) rose & said, he felt specially glad to see one friend with them because he remembered "when a stripling" Elizabeth Robson's first visit in the midst of their terrible trials. "She was a skilful woman of God who could throw a stone to a hairs breadth & never miss & never hurt or hit a friend but always hit a foe" & he was exceedingly glad to welcome her grandson among them, & much more to the same effect. After dinner was the Representative meeting (Meeting for Sufferings) at which a good deal of business was done & the Committee to assist R. W. Douglas & his family appointed, which it was decided, I should meet with. Spent the evening in the drawingroom with the young Coffins & their wives, in interesting conversation some hymns & closed by prayer from me & address by Dr. Thomas.

4th day 26th Devotional meeting at 8:30 very solemn & nice. The Yearly Meeting began at 10 o'clk. All our Certificates to listen to again which is rather wearying. Then our London General Epistle & all the Epistles. 6000 of ours ordered to be printed. Glad to see the most wonderful quaker preacher in the united States come into meeting, David Updegraff of Mount Pleasant Ohio. An epistle was received from the separated body who call themselves Western Yearly Meeting, but not read. At dinner we were

---

[4] Timothy Nicholson (1828–1924) was a most important Friend in Indiana Yearly Meeting for decades. Born in North Carolina, he moved to Indiana in 1855, was active in the Richmond Conference of 1887, supported Earlham College, and many other concerns. Walter C. Woodward, *Timothy Nicholson, Master Quaker* (Richmond, Ind., 1927); *DAB; H-DQB.*

joined at C. F. Coffins by dear Hannah W. Smith whose acquaintance I am particularly glad to make. Afternoon the Tract & Bible Meeting principally occupied by Stanley Pumphrey in a very interesting lecture on the Bible. After that came home to tea, where I was very pleased to meet Murray Shipley & his wife from Cincinatti.[5] A meeting for worship in the evening opened by prayer from Dr. Thomas. Then I spoke & Dr. Thomas added a few words. D. Updegraff followed, speaking for an hour & 1/2—the most marvellous sermon in some ways I ever heard. It was on the words, "unto you it is given on the behalf of Christ, not only to believe on His name but also to suffer with Him." He closed in prayer, after a hymn & a few words from

---

[5] Murray Shipley (1830–1899) retired from business at the age of thirty-five, and dedicated himself to Quaker concerns. He was instrumental in beginning the mission in Mexico, shared in the Indian work under President Grant, and worked for prison reform. He was a brother of Hannah S. Bean (q.v.). *American Friend* **6** (1899): p. 107. H-DQB.

Fig. 3. Friends gathering for Indiana Yearly Meeting at the old meeting-house built in 1822. (Drawing by Marcus Mote, 1817–1898.)

Fig. 4. New meetinghouse at Richmond, Indiana, under construction in 1877. The contrast in architecture with the earlier building suggests the changing pattern in mid-western Quakerism.

E. Mallinson. It is a mile walk from here to meeting. I generally walk, but C.F.C. is most kind, always sending his carriage & buggie backwards & forwards as often as anyone wants to use it. This morning, before meeting he took Dr. Thomas & me to see the new meetinghouse which only wants the roof & fittings. It is a really handsome building, red brick, with towers at one end, in the best part of the city of Richmond, a pretty place of some 15000 persons. It is intensely hot again & my dearest Tenie in her letter received today, tells of fires at home & winter curtains!

5th day 27th At 8.30 the adjourned meeting of Ministers & Elders. Stanley P. Dr. Thomas & I asked for a meeting for ministers only, & it is fixed for tomorrow evening. The state of Society as brought before that meeting, was discussed & I was greatly helped to speak to it. Y. Meeting at 10. I was liberated to visit the Women's meeting which I did. Micajah Binford, an Elder going with me, & much satisfaction was expressed afterwards. An appeal case was brought up & referred to a Committee, of Walter Egerton who was disowned for publishing a pamphlet which was sent to me at home last year, I think. We shall hear the result tomorrow.[6] Then we had a long discussion on the payment of Ministers & a large Committee appointed to report next year. I was asked to give my views which I did at some length on the difference between preaching for pay & being paid for preaching. I hope there will be some very practical issue, for there are many earnest ministers in these Western meetings who are very poor men. They devote their lives to preaching & leave their poor wives & children quite unprovided for, only depending on the chance kindness of friends & often get hopelessly in debt.[7] Driven out to a lovely house, Francis Evans to dine, Dr. & Mrs Thompson,[8] H. W. Smith & the Shipleys also there, & D. Updegraff & to my no small welcome Anthony Kimber has arrived to attend this Yearly Meeting. Had a deeply interesting dinner spirtually. Home mission meeting occupied the afternoon, at which I spoke, & H. W. Smith gave us a delightful Bible lesson from Ezra & Nehemiah then S.P. & others spoke & finally an Indian Methodist preached, one of the Oneida tribe. His name is Sunrise alias Thomas S. Dana. He spoke excellently. Tea at home, sitting by dear H. W. Smith a lovely Christian, on one side & Rhoda Coffin, a no less sweet saintly lady on the other. Truly at this Yearly Meeting, the lines are fallen unto me in pleasant places. I only want my dearest Tenie to enjoy

[6] Walter Edgerton (b. 1806) was the author of a pamphlet entitled, *Modern Quakerism Examined and Contrasted with that of the Ancient Type* (n.p., 1876), and reprinted in England with an introduction from William Pitt. Earlier in his career he had supported the anti-slavery group in Indiana, and had been disowned at that time as well. H-DQB.

[7] *Friends Review* noted that W. R. spoke on this subject, emphasizing the difference between preaching for pay, and being paid for preaching. **31** (1877): p. 124.

[8] He probably means Dr. and Mrs. James C. Thomas.

the blessings temporal & spiritual with me. Meeting for Worship at 7.30 H.W.S. very excellent. I followed & then D. Updegraff with great power & when those who wished to consecrate themselves to the Lord were asked to rise, they rose in all parts of the house & the power of the Lord was with us of a truth.

6th day 28th The meeting with the ministers only, proved very solemn & interesting & was finally adjourned till 7.30 this evening. The Y.M. met at 10 & was occupied on the state of the Society, on which I had a good deal to say.[9] 18000 members now belong to this Y. Meeting. Dined at a dear old Friend's named Elizabeth Hopkins, where Deborah Thomas is lodging. A large Temperance Meeting occupied the afternoon, at which, by request, I said a little. The ministers meeting in evening was very solemn & intensely interesting. The great & blessed truth of the real *death* of the body of sin—the old man—was freely discussed, experiences were called for & freely & simply given, & the old doctrine of the subjugation of sin *not* its annihilation was also discussed. Broke up at 10.30 & I escorted H. W. Smith home. I should be ungrateful if I did not acknowledge the great blessing to my own soul, association with this holy woman & her no less holy & gifted sister Mary Thomas, is more & more, every day. Truly they live in the power of God.

7th day 29th The dry heat has produced such a state of dust as I have only seen in Australia. The whole air is full of dust & ones white garments require frequent washing. Wrote & posted a letter to my dear cousin J. J. Neave this morning. Meeting of ministers & elders so crowded with religious exercises, that there was only time to pass a certificate for R. W. Douglas before we had to adjourn. Y.

---

[9] He spoke once more on the question of the paid ministry, and the danger of a person going into a meeting expecting to preach. He said, "if our meetings are held in the power of God, it will matter little what minister is present." *Friends Review* **31** (1877): p. 137.

Meeting at 10. State of Society concluded.[10] A young American minister asked, (but was not liberated) to visit the Women's meeting. Earlham College report discussed. Dined at home. Chloe Taylor & her husband (three weeks married) met us there. She is J. H. Douglas's daughter. Afternoon. Firstday school conference—very interesting—specially H. W. Smith. Evening, educational conference. I did not attend it, but staid to be present at a drawingroom meeting at C. F. Coffins conducted by H.W.S.—deeply instructive & opening the way for some very earnest discourse between me & Charles Henry & his Flora Coffin, the latter a member of the Swedenborgian church.

1st day 9th mo: 30th A very thrilling devotional meeting at 8. Large & earnest *con*fessions & *pro*fessions from all parts of the house. At 10 o'clk the meetings for Worship. I will send the newspaper announcements of the arrangements for the division of ministers, which was closely adhered to by us all. The scene was very wonderful. Train after train arriving at the depot, crowded with passengers, the streets near & the meetinghouse ground, full of vehicles, the roads lined with refreshment stalls, all teetotal, the one great centre of attraction being the two meeting houses & the preaching stand in the grounds. I suppose 10 to 15 thousand would be present altogether. Our meeting was opened by prayer by James Bailey.[11] E. Mallinson read & prayed. Then I spoke for a long while & was followed by Dr. Thomas, & then his dear stepmother Deborah Thomas. Then E. Mallinson very powerfully & Dr. Thomas engaged in prayer. A quieter meeting is not remembered & I hear

10 The *Christian Worker* reported that W. R. spoke to the young men in the meeting, urging them to maintain the Quaker reputation for "honesty, and integrity in business relations. He would not give anything for a religion that did not make men better in all the relations of life." 7 (1877): p. 662.

11 James E. Bailey (1810?–1880) was born in Virginia, but his family soon moved to Ohio. He was recorded as a minister in 1855, and moved to Iowa five years later. He had just moved on to Kansas in 1880 when he died there. *Friends Review* 34 (1880): p. 233.

the others report the same of theirs. Home to dinner, then back again to meeting. J.H.D. Dr. Thomas & I, on the preaching stand. Here we were all greatly favored & many wept. Hundreds of black faces among the white people. Of course we all roared as loud as we could so as to reach as many of the thousands as possible & I am glad to hear were very well heard. In my opening prayer, I earnestly prayed for loud clear voices, & my prayer was graciously heard. The young Coffins & their wives & dear H.W.S. accompanied me to the Presbyterian church where I was wonderfully helped to preach to the most aristocratic audience in the most stylish church in Richmond. After the service closed, I gave H.W.S. my arm & we hurried off to the Friends meetinghouse where a scene of indescribable solemnity was being acted "an Altar of prayer." Friends old & young, smart & very plain, kneeling in rows, sometimes quite still, often ejaculating short earnest prayer for a baptism of the Holy Ghost, some praising God with a loud voice that their prayers were answered. Dear David Updegraff & J.H.D. quietly moving about among the kneeling throng, sometimes in prayer themselves & at others quietly whispering words of comfort or of counsel. I never realized such agonising in prayer before. It was a scene never to be forgotten. Did not get home till past 11 o'clk, tired, but very thankful for a day of uncommon blessing. I enclose two cuttings from one of the Richmond Papers which please preserve carefully, as I cannot replace them. We are truly public property in this land. I may report myself in good health, but rather exhausted with the great heat which does not decrease yet.

2nd day 10th Mo: 1st Meeting of Ministers & Elders, a time of much earnest religious exercise. Yearly Meeting at 10 o'clk. The heat so great today that it was a real endurance to sit meeting. Principally occupied with reports of educational work, & the work in Tennessee among the poor white & black people, reports from Elkanah Beard, Alida Clark &c.[12] Dined at Isaac Evans with a large party of Friends. In the afternoon gave to the Yearly meeting a long detail of Mission work in the South Sea Islands, a thing I felt very reluctant to do, but the newspapers having described me in connection with such work, friends insisted on it & the shutters were raised so as to have the great house full. Accompanied Dr. & Mary Thomas & H. W. Smith to Frank & Flora Coffins. They have a lovely house in the country. In again to the evening meeting—a very solemn time—many kneeling at the "Altar of Prayer." This was after E. Mallinson, H. W. Smith, her sister & I had spoken very earnestly.

3rd day 10th mo 2nd Yesterday was the hottest day at Richmond they had all the summer 93° in the shade all day & only 2 degrees less to day. It is the hottest Indiana Y. Meeting in the memory of Friends. Closing meeting of Ministers & Elders this morning, a very cordial expression of thankfulness expressed by Charles Coffin & echoed all round the meeting for my visit & labours. I spoke & afterwards closed in prayer. At the Yearly Meeting was a very interesting report of work done by Friends, among the Indians, also Mission work in Mexico, &c. &c.—a long sitting, but lively. A committee to revise the Book of Discipline, a Peace meeting in the afternoon I did not attend, but spent at home with my dear friends the Coffins. The Pumphreys, H. W. Smith & the Thomas's accompanied me to Charles Edward & Flora Coffins to tea & I staid the

---

[12] Elkanah Beard (1833–1905) dedicated most of his life to Quaker service in one way or another. He was born in Indiana, married Irene Johnson, and gave much time to caring for soldiers during the Civil War. He also worked for the Freedmen after the war, and with the American Indians. He and his wife went to India as missionaries for three years in 1869, and in 1882 traveled in the ministry in Europe. *American Friend* **12** (1905): p. 182. L-DQB.

Alida Clark (1822?–1892), the wife of Calvin Clark, who had shared with him the direction of Southland College since 1864. They were members of Indiana Yearly Meeting, but lived in Arkansas. *Friends Review* **45** (1892): p. 605.

evening with them, while the others went to the evening
Devotional meeting, I wishing to have some religious conversation especially with Flora who is a Swedenborgian
the daughter of a Physician. A letter from my dearest Tenie
with good news of my darlings at home is fresh cause of
thankfulness to God.

4th day 10th mo: 3rd At 8. this morning Joseph Moore
president of Earlham College called for me & drove me out
to Earlham, where he shewed me over this very interesting
establishment where about 200 young men & women receive a very high class of education.[13] They have excellent
library & museum. The college is the property of Indiana
Yearly Meeting. At 8.30. the Students were all assembled in
their meetinghouse where after the President had read a
Psalm I prayed & preached to them, feeling great liberty,
though I dreaded this visit very much, because of the high
intellectual attainments of the congregation. The closing
sitting of the Y.M was a good deal occupied in routine work,
reports, epistles &c. Stanley P. & Dr. Thomas went into the
Women's meeting & Deborah Thomas came into our meeting when the business was concluded. I spoke a few
minutes & after prayer Indiana Yearly Meeting closed.
Home to dinner, & spent the afternoon partly at home &
with Stanley at the Photographers who desired us to sit for
our portraits that he might have them for sale. Stanley,
Sarah & I went to tea at William & Lydia Coffins. They
have a sweet little home, a sweet little baby boy & are
dear little christian people.

5th day 10th mo 4th One of the principal manufactures
of Richmond is that of coffins. There is one establishment
here that annually sends out a hundred thousand.[14] The

---

[13] Joseph Moore (1832–1905) had studied at Harvard, and taught science
much of his life. He was recorded as a minister in 1865. After a time as
president of Earlham, he went to the New Garden (N.C.) boarding school which
became Guilford College. *Quaker Biog.*, ser. II, **4**: p. 3. H-DQB.
[14] The J. M. Hutton & Co. firm was founded in 1868.

summer heat came to an end this morning with a high wind & to day is quite cool. Rose at 5 o'clk, found breakfast all ready for me, & the carriage to take me to the Depot. Daniel Hill, his wife & some other Friends met me there & we took the cars, 80 miles to the great city of Cincinatti, the largest city in Ohio with a population of 400.000. Murray Shipley met me here at the depot & drove me to his house, to a second breakfast. Then to meeting where were the Thomas party & H. W. Smith. I opened in prayer, then Dr. Thomas & his wife & H.W.S. spoke briefly. I followed, Daniel Hill said a few words & Deborah Thomas offered a very long & beautiful prayer. Several short experiences were given & we broke up. M. Shipley took Dr. Thomas & me to look over the Hospital with its 500 patients, considered one of the most perfect in the world. After dinner we went a lovely drive up on to the range of lofty hills which form the beautiful background to Cincinatti. Took tea at Maurice & Hannah White's. The latter is C. F. Coffin's sister. They are very wealthy & their house is one mass of luxury. Maurice took me in his carriage to the meetinghouse where a meeting was held at my appointment for the public—very solemn but not very large. M. Shipley closed it in prayer. The meetinghouse is a pretty one, carpeted all over & seated with handsome Walnut benches.

6th day 10th mo: 5th Had a long religious talk with dear Murray & Katherine Shipley, people of rare intellectual & spiritual attainments. M.S. drove me to see a fountain in the city acknowledged to be the finest in the world, designed at Munich. Also a suspension bridge half a mile long (missing 300 feet) over the Ohio river, the largest in the world. Then to a childrens home—deeply interesting—managed by M.S. After dinner, K.S. & I called on dear old Harriet Steer, a minister aged 83 very bright & full of heavenly love. After tea, the whole meeting was invited to meet me in M. Shipley's drawingroom & many came, but I do not quite like to be the lion of the drawingroom, however I sought to improve the occasion & did so, I believe, to the honor of God. Closed by reading & prayer.

7th day 10th mo: 6th Rose at about 6 o'clk & my dear host & hostess were both at breakfast with me. Left Cincinatti by train at 7 A.M. in quite a sharp frost, so that the great stoves in the cars were lighted. Reached Richmond at 11, Elijah Coffin meeting me at the depot & driving me to his father's home where Rhoda Coffin gave me a very warm welcome & I had a long chat with her. Went to Coffins Bank & had some pleasant converse with Elijah, Charles & William. Dined at Elijah & Elma Coffins & then it was fixed much to my satisfaction, that Elma & her cousin Mariana Ladd, should accompany me to Spiceland. M. Ladd is a girl of 22, niece of Isabella Jones & also of Charles F. Coffins. Left Richmond at about 3 o'clk in the cars for Dunreath; where William Egerton met us & took us to his house to tea. Then in two conveyances, we went to Spiceland & took up our abode at Clarkson Davis's. He is away, but his wife very kindly offered us beds. Spiceland is a very large meeting. I believe it is the largest meeting of Friends in the world. 800 members or thereabouts, besides the great Academy of 200 children & adults, of which Clarkson Penrose is Professor.[15] Dear Rufus King is not yet here, so I fear I shall miss him altogether. He is one of 12 recorded ministers belonging to Spiceland. It is quite a small village & $\frac{3}{4}$ of the population are Friends. They have a fine new meetinghouse seating nearly 1000 & it was well filled this evening, to hear me lecture on Mission work in the South seas. &c.

---

[15] Clarkson Davis (1833–1883) was born in Indiana and spent most of his life there. Since he was the head of the Spiceland Academy, and had been since 1863, one assumes that W. R. made a mistake in referring to him the second time as Clarkson Penrose. There had been a Clarkson Penrose attending Iowa Yearly Meeting. *Friends Review* **36** (1883): p. 729; *Minutes of Iowa Yearly Meeting of Friends*, 1877: p. 1.

1st day 10th mo: 7th The great meetinghouse full from end to end. A dear minister offered prayer—Caleb Johnson.[16] Then I spoke for a full hour & prayed & a dear woman minister closed in prayer—a very solemn blessed meeting, as many testified. My self & companions went to dinner at the house of two dear old Friends Solomon & Priscilla Macey's & then were driven out to visit a dear aged friend Hannah Unthank who has kept her bed with paralysis for nearly 4 years.[17] She is great Aunt to my companions. It was a sweet lesson to us to sit by her bed, & see the support Jesus gives in such affliction. Her husband is bed-ridden in another room. His mind as well as body is wrong. One daughter attends to both, pretty fully. I read & prayed with this dear aged woman before we came away. Tea at Taylor's whose son Jacob lives with him. Jacob has a young bride, Chloe, daughter of J. H. Douglas. It has at last begun to rain in torrents so that our evening meeting was small—perhaps about 500, but very favored & I took leave of Spiceland meeting & Friends, with a very thankful heart. Returned to our quarters at the Davis's. I must post this in the morning as I have two meetings fixed for me, & W. Egerton is to call for me at 8:30. to drive me to Rich Square to a meeting there, at 10. Then I am to be driven on to Raysville, I believe, to a meeting there in the evening. Then on 3rd day, I go on to Indianapolis, join Stanley & Sarah Pumphrey there & take the cars for the long Western journey over the prairies & the great river to Kansas, where the P.'s & I are to be the guests of Frank A. Wright, during the Yearly Meeting.

[16] Caleb Johnson (1821?–1898) was born in North Carolina, but his family migrated to the Spiceland region when he was quite young. He was recorded as a minister in 1865, conducted evangelistic work, and served as a pastor of several meetings. *American Friend* **5** (1898): p. 428.

[17] Anna (Hiatt) Unthank and her husband Eli were both born in North Carolina, and married there before migrating to the Spiceland area of Indiana. They both died in the spring of 1881 when Anna Unthank was in her eightieth year and her husband nearly eighty-two. *Friends Review* **34** (1881): p. 665.

2nd day 10th mo: 8th Rose this morning to find it a soaking wet day. Took leave of my kind hostess Hannah Davis at 8.30. & of the kind travelling companions from Richmond, Elma Coffin & Mariana Ladd who return there this morning, William Egerton calling for me in his carriage. He is son of Walter Egerton whose appeal was heard at Indiana Yearly Meeting, disowned for writing that offensive pamphlet that was sent us at my dear home. William is very unlike his father, having become a thoroughly con-verted man. He drove me 8 miles to Rich Square a wooden meetinghouse in the forest, most beautifully situated. Here, though it was secondday morning & very wet, at 10 o'clk nearly 200 Friends assembled & we had a very solemn, blessed time. Then to John Macey's to dine & then W.E. drove me 12 miles to Knightstown & Raysville, two little towns not a mile apart, each possessing a meeting of Friends. Had tea at Benaiah Parker's & then to a meeting appointed for me in the Methodist Chapel at Raysville, being larger than the meetinghouse. Had a good meeting, many not Friends there, as well as Knightstown & Raysville Friends. Charles Hubbard, a minister took me to his house to lodge.[18] He is a gentleman, a member of Congress, born with only one arm. I have met him, both at Western & Indiana Y.M. I sat talking with him, his wife, her aged mother & his girls for a long while, before retiring to rest. A day to be very thankful for! It feels to me a very serious thing to appoint meetings as Friends are doing for me. They come in hundreds, driving several miles to be present, wet or fine & one feels as if one ought to have some specially good food to set before them, for they come to hear the English Friend preach. But I have no reason to believe any have gone away disappointed.

---

[18] Charles Hubbard was not a member of the Congress of the United States. W. R. evidently is referring to the Indiana legislature.

VI. Kansas Yearly Meeting

3rd day 9th October After breakfast C. Hubbard took
me to call on an aged friend & his wife, the latter confined
to her bed for 37 years—a patient sufferer! The former
[,] Nathan Parker, was for months the companion of my
grandmother in North Carolina. Thence to the depot,
where I took the cars to Indianapolis, & arriving there, was
met by William Evans & Stanley & Sarah Pumphrey who
escorted me to W. Evans's house to dine. Thence, back to
the depot & here we were joined by Wilson Spray & Isaac
Jay (Allens father) bound as *we* were for Kansas.[1] Left
Indianapolis at 1 o'clk P.M. & when it became dark we got
the conductor to bring us a table & we had a very interesting
Bible lesson from John 10 chap. At about 9 o'clk reached
the city of St. Louis a great place of half a million inhabitants, on the banks of the Mississippi. The river here is
very wide, having received into it the waters of the Missouri about 100 miles north.[2] The bridge over the river at
St. Louis has only been completed (I think) two years & is
renowned as the grandest bridge in the world. Over the
railway bridge is one for carriages & foot passengers. The
trains go over very slowly for fear of any ill effects from
vibration. Then a tunnel runs under the city & we enter
the state of Missouri. Changed trains at St. Louis & took
sleeping berths on a Pulman car.

4th day 10th mo: 10th Rose at about 7 o'clk, & stopped
at a wayside station for breakfast. From there, the ride is
lovely, for probably 50 miles close to the river Missouri
which though very muddy is a majestic stream & the banks

---

[1] Isaac Jay (1811–1880) was born in Ohio, and married Rhoda Cooper (1813–
1894). He was recorded as a minister in 1850, and moved to Indiana at about
the same time. He visited Friends all over America, and felt he should do
so at his own expense. *Autobiography of Allen Jay.*

[2] Ten miles north of St. Louis would be closer to the facts.

richly wooded, the trees just turning into their grand Autumn tints, for which America is so justly celebrated. At 10 o'clk reached Kansas City where we had to change, & met on the platform H. Balkwill & her companion & Elkanah & Irene Beard bound also to Kansas Y. Meeting. Reached Lawrence about 2 o'clk, & the Pumphreys and I are comfortably located at Frank A. Wrights. He has been married about 6 weeks to Mary Chase, called for distinction "Daisy." Jane Wright lives with them & looks very well & younger than in England.[3] After dinner I left the Pumphreys to rest & walked up a steep hill behind the house, from which is an exquisite view over the city of Lawrence, & the miles of Prairie beyond. The Kansas river winds very prettily through the city & trees planted everywhere give a nice effect, but the place is thoroughly Yankie in its streets, stores & get up. After tea, called on Washington Hadley, where Helen B. & her companion & David Hunt &c. are located. Called also on Enoch Hoag, one of the most devoted to the work among the Indians. My bed is made up on a sofa in the parlour & I slept well on it. J. Wright is not strong. She suffers constantly from Neuralgia in one foot, but is very lively & much interested in [Saffron] Walden news.

5th day 10th mo. 11th Walked to the Bank at which Frank is clerk. He took me on to the roof to see the view, which is charming. Sat in the Bank parlour with Dr. Nicholson & then went to his home to see E. & I. Beard.[4] After dinner, went to the meetinghouse. It is a very fine stone building. My dear ones will remember William Coffin

[3] Jane (Fisher) Wright (1819?–1888) was born in Ireland, and married to Henry Wright of Middlesborough, England, a draper who died in 1849. The *Friend* (London) **28** (1888): p. 104.

[4] William Nicholson (1826–1899) was born in North Carolina and lived there through the Civil War. He was a physician who studied at the University of Pennsylvania. In 1870 he moved to Lawrence, Kansas, and held important positions in the Indian work. A recorded minister, he was clerk of Kansas Yearly Meeting. H–DQB.

FIG. 5. Friends gathering in front of the meetinghouse at yearly meeting time at Lawrence, Kansas. (Undated photograph thought to be from the 1870's.)

being at S. Walden at the second Quarterly Meeting held there, to beg some money for building it. It is now I think out of debt. The meeting of M's & E's at 2 P.M. Minutes read for W.R. Sarah Pumphrey—Helen B. & Susan D. from our side the Atlantic, & for D. Updegraff & his beloved sister, Sarah Jenkins from Ohio, also William L. George from Western Y.M. & W. Spray from the same. Isaac Jay, David Hunt & Sarah B. Henshaw.[5] Answers to Queries & then some long & earnest addresses from W. Spray & David

[5] The Yearly Meeting Minutes refer to a Hannah Hinshaw from Iowa, rather than Sarah B; mention Adelbert Wood from Ohio, and list Elkanah and Irene Beard from Indiana, already referred to by W.R. *Minutes of Kansas Yearly Meeting of Friends*, 1877: p. 31.

Updegraff & his sister. Several prayers & short communications closed the sitting. I went to tea at Washington Hadley's, where are D.U. & S.J., H.B. & S. Doyle and dear little Mary Rogers who has recently come to reside in Kansas Y.M. 20 miles from here.[6] Spent an evening of intense interest, conversing principally with D.U. Came home about 10 o'clk to find letters from my own dearest Tenie & my precious sister Priscie. Sat up in my parlour bedroom by the fire, reading & enjoying, & thanking God for them & the good news they bring me, as if in answer to D.U.'s earnest prayer at parting, this evening.

6th day 12th Devotional Meeting at 8.30. I prayed & then spoke considerably, as did D. Updegraff, in perfect harmony. At 10 o'clk the regular meeting for worship was held upstairs. Stanley & D. Hunt prayed, then I spoke a long while in great liberty, Stanley followed, then a thorough Wilburite, very painfully.[7] D.U. spoke with much power & then asked for silent prayer, & while some of us were kneeling, the same friend replied most tryingly, to D.U. M. Rogers sang a hymn sweetly, a woman rose & protested against a Friend "singing a song out of a book," a woman minister prayed, & we broke up. There is a fearful amount of the Wilbur element in this, the newest, & I fear the weakest, of the American Y.M.'s. Dined at W. Hadley's & then turned back again to attend the opening sitting of the Y. Meeting. This was on the whole, satisfactory, but much taken up with routine. Two years ago, they decided never to give returning Minutes, but D.U. brought up the

---

[6] Washington Hadley (1817–1911) was born in North Carolina, and moved to Indiana when thirteen. He moved to Lawrence, Kansas, in 1866, and remained there until 1893 when he transferred to Whittier, California. He was at one time clerk of Kansas Yearly Meeting, was the benefactor of Whittier College in its early days, and was a banker for more than fifty years. *American Friend* **19** (1912): p. 38.

[7] W. R. spoke from a text in the Psalms, on the "work of regeneration and cleansing of the heart, . . . in a very forcible manner." *Friends Review* **31** (1877): p. 169.

subject, which led to a long and animated discussion, & finally resulted in a Committee being appointed to do so, with a full understanding that they should express on such returning Minutes just what they feel, whether satisfactory or otherwise. I believe the plan had been abandoned just to cover the want of unity in the church.[8] Home to tea, where I met Mary White, her two children & her husband. Those who remember her in Walden as the almost snow white daughter of Jane Wright would hardly recognise her in the hard working little farmer's wife who milks cows, cooks dinners, feeds the pigs, & cares for her little ones. Went to a meeting for worship again in the evening, where S.P. & I had the principal service, Helen B. saying a few sweet words. I was in mercy, enabled to reach the conditions of two in the meeting who rose at the close & said so, publicly. I must post this in the morning to insure its not missing the mail home. I expect to leave here for Baltimore on 3rd day evening, travelling as far as Cincinatti, in about 33 hours right on. Then as the trains do not fit, I intend to stay at Cincinatti till the following evening & then 24 hours on to Baltimore, reaching there on 6th day night. I may report myself well in health though rather exhausted by a sudden return of heat today, ushered in by a thunderstorm last night.

7th day 10th mo: 13th Devotional Meeting at 8.30. A time *promising* much blessing, but marred at the close, by a long declamatory address from a minister named Cyrus Harvey of strong Wilbur tendencies who cannot bear the

---

[8] The Minute referred to, approved in 1875, on returning minutes for visiting ministers included the following: the "way has not opened to pursue the usual mode of separate returning minutes to ministers in attendance, and after careful consideration of the whole subject, we are united in proposing that hereafter the Clerk make a general minute, including the names and position of all those in attendance, . . . and on application of any one interested, the Clerk be directed to furnish a copy of said Minute." *Minutes of Kansas Yearly Meeting of Friends*, 1875: p. 43.

plain preaching of sanctification & Holy Ghost baptism.[9]
His sermon alluded to having these doctrines "dinned
forever in their ears, making the young people profess what
they knew nothing about, while the older ones who have
lived the life of Christians by obeying the inner light, are
thought little of." His discourse just seemed to pull back
the blessing which was coming. Thus do we Friends pay
the penalty of our liberty "to relieve our minds." Yearly
Meeting at 10 o'clk, our London General & New York
Epistles read. Answers to the queries read & then S.P. &
I gave full & long addresses on the state of the Society,
much apparently, to the comfort of Friends. I dined at
Dr. William Nicholson's. He is clerk to the Y.M. & a very
excellent man, a minister. He says that Frank Wright is
one of the most useful men in Lawrence meeting—superintendent of their Sabbath schools &c. I think the Gibsons
will like to know this. In the afternoon, S.P. gave his address on the Bible. Took tea at Dr. Stewards with the
P.'s & D.U. Then to meeting again, to a meeting of "Ministers & all workers for Jesus," convened at my request &
united in by Stanley P. We both spoke a long while & I
believe the presence & power of the Lord were with us.
Had some very plain things to say to some of them, but
speaking in love, it was received in love also.

1st day 14th A soaking wet morning. Only those who
have seen a city built in the prairie, the *roads* not made but
only beaten down by traffic, can quite understand the state
of rich black mud which prevails everywhere when it rains
& turns the beaten roads into a ploughed field of heavy
loam soil & such we had to walk through to meeting this
morning where ever we had the roads to cross. The paths

---

[9] Cyrus Harvey (1843–1916) was born in Indiana, and served in the Union
army during the Civil War. After that he married, moved to Kansas and began
to teach. He was recorded as a minister in 1875, and led the Wilburite group
in Kansas, which separated from the older yearly meeting in 1880. The *Friend*
(Phila.) **90** (1916): p. 53. H-DQB.

are of wood like Oskaloosa. I conducted the Devotional meeting at 8.45. Many most wonderful & interesting experiences were given. At 10. began meeting for worship at both houses. S.P. &c. were upstairs; H.B. & I were downstairs. W. Spray asked for quiet; then H.B. prayed & I spoke a long while. While I was speaking & many were in tears & a most solemn feeling was over us, a plain old man friend rose & said nearly these words "Friends, I wish we might now have a really solemn sermon in the life, instead of this light lifeless talk which only causes levity." I keep very calm & "sweet inside," for which I bless my blessed Master but physically these things always make me tremble, but a sort of whispered, "go on dear brother" reassured me & I proceeded. David Hunt & W. Spray followed & the old man left the meeting. We certainly had a good time. I found afterwards that the same man had openly opposed Helen B. in a meeting she had here before Y.M. Dined at Enoch Hoag's. He is one of the most earnest Indian workers & has others likeminded with him.[10] He called a Modoc girl to sing hymns. Went to meeting again after dinner, dear D. Updegraff occupied almost all the time, except that I opened it in prayer. He preached a glorious sermon full of power & of the Holy Ghost. Several were converted. Had tea at my quarters & Dr. & Mrs. Steward called & escorted me through the mud to the Congregational chapel—the best congregation in Lawrence. I was greatly helped in preaching; but the singing was sadly formal & all done by a choir. I have been much pleased to meet Albert Alexander, who is here for Y.M. He has a farm at Touganoxy, 13 miles from here & he seemed

---

[10] Enoch Hoag (1812?–1884) had a strong concern for both the Freedmen and the Indians. He was in Iowa after 1854, and in 1869 was named by President Grant to be Superintendent of Indian Affairs in the Central district. In his later life he was recorded as a minister, and died in New Hampshire. Rayner Kelsey, *Friends and the Indians* (Philadelphia, 1917); *Friends Review* 37 (1884): p. 809.

settled there, at present. He rather hopes Bernard will return from Australia this way so as to visit him.

2nd day 10th mo: 15th Heavy rain again all day. Meeting of M's & E.'s in the morning—a good time, I believe. Y.M. at 10 o'clk. Dear David Hunt & I paid a blessed visit to the Womens meeting. I am told that as soon as we left it, a dear aged woman minister Penelope Gardner rose, & expressed her thankfulness for the address of the young brother & that she remembered hearing his Grandmother preach the same sermon on the same text 40 years ago. D.U. the Pumphreys & I dined at John B. Miles'.[11] He is agent for some of the Indian tribes. We paid him & his, a very interesting visit. Albert Alexander & William Coffin came to tea with us. In the evening, a youth's meeting was held at the request of D.U. S.P. & W.R., but with the exception of prayers from both of us, we left the service to D.U. who spoke for $1\frac{1}{2}$ hours, very beautifully & afterwards many rose for prayer, many confessed their Saviour & we had a very memorable time.

3rd day 16th Went into the principal street of the city to secure a seat in the Omnibus. Then to a meeting of Indian workers held at the request of S.P. & W.R.—a very interesting time. Many of these are attending this Y.M., as Kansas & the Indian territory join & Friends are the most successful workers among this down trodden people. A painful scene was meanwhile enacted downstairs at the devotional meeting. A minister (Cyrus Harvey) loudly declaiming against D.U. & his teaching & at last a recorded minister (a woman) went to him & said—"we read of a deceiver & an antichrist & thou art the man." The Y.M. began at 10 o'clk, the report of the Committe on the two Epistles from the Western Y.M. was brought in & adopted,

---

[11] John D. Miles continued his work with the Indians until 1884. After his wife Lucy died in 1892 he moved from Lawrence, Kansas, to Antlers, in the Indian Territory for a decade. Kelsey, *Friends and the Indians*.

tho' C. Harvey said, if doctrine & not law had anything to do with the decision it would have been reversed. Then the returning Minutes were produced. One for S.P. & one for me, but they refused to give our American brother any. I ventured a protest & told them that while I thanked them for mine, I would rather give mine to D.U. as if I had been blessed to them, he had been much more so, but it was of no use. The Wilbur element is in power & they have no unity with D.U. The meeting adjourned at about 1.30. I gave them a very earnest parting sermon which seemed to have some weight. It took me nearly ½ an hour to shake Friends by the hand & say 'farewell.' David Hunt said, "Walter, I thank our dear Saviour, that He sent thee here, & for the precious unity I have with thee." S. & S. Pumphrey & H.B. & S.Doyle I shall not probably see again till they return home. I feel parting with Stanley. I have sat by his side during 4 Y.M.'s & we have laboured together in perfect harmony. The Y.M. will not close without two more sittings, but I could hardly get to Baltimore in time for Y.M. there, if I did not leave to day, & I am very weary bodily & mentally. After a hasty dinner at F. Wright's, the buss called & took me through the mud to the depot which I left at about 3. & much enjoyed the ride from Lawrence to Kansas City about 40 miles, close by the side of the pretty Kansas river. At Kansas city, got a cup of tea & changed train, securing a berth in a "Pulman." The night was very warm, & to make bad matters worse, the car was heated throughout with hot water pipes, so that sleep seemed just impossible.

4th day 17th Arrived at St. Louis just at daylight & here stopped an hour & had breakfast. Then on again through the great tunnel under St. Louis & on to the grand bridge on which I crossed once more the Mississippi, the 4th & (I trust) the last time. It always feels nearer to home to be east of this mighty river. Rode on the platform at the

back of the train to get a good idea of the bridge. It cost
with its approaches &c. ten million dollars, ruining three
companies that undertook it. 20 minutes for dinner at
Terra Haute & then on to Indianapolis. Here again
changed & took cars for Cincinatti where I arrived at 11
o'clk at night, weary & sleepy. Went to the "Grand Hotel"
a noble place, where a "lift" soon deposited me on the floor
on which my room was & I was soon asleep. I have greatly
admired the fine Autumn tints to day. They far exceed
anything I have ever seen, richest red & purple, bright
orange, yellow, green, some nearly white & some very dark.
I longed for my nature loving friends at home to share the
feast with me & remembered how dear Aunt P. Green
admired the American autumn.[12] This heat just commenced
again is what they call their Indian summer.

    5th day 18th   Did not breakfast till 8 this morning, having
enjoyed the luxury of a good wash very much. Wrote a
note & posted it to my precious wife & then sallied forth to
the meetinghouse where a very warm welcome awaited
me & I found, to my surprise, it was Monthly meeting, but
no meeting is joined. It is only Cincinatti meeting. I
preached a long while & Murray Shipley prayed. My certificates were asked for & read. I am getting weary of hearing
them—the 11th time in America. Friends say, I look weary
& worn & Dr. Taylor wrote me a Prescription for quinine
pills which M.S. at once procured me. Drove off to dinner
with Hannah White, C.F. Coffins sister. Her niece Marianna Ladd is with her & is to go to Baltimore with me. Her
father (a minister) is to be at that Y.M. After tea in this most
luxurious establishment, Morris White drove his wife, M.
Ladd & me to the depot, where we took leave of them &
were soon in the Pulman's car, where we each retired to

---

[12] Priscilla Green (1802–1877) had come from England to travel in the
ministry in America in 1856 and stayed some two years. She was a sister of
W.R.'s mother. *Ann. Mon.,* n.s., **37**: p. 78. H-DQB.

rest behind our own curtain. The night was very hot &
the car heated nearly to suffocation, so that refreshing
sleep was an impossibility to me.

6th day 19th Rose about 6.30 & found we had just
reached a scene of surpassing beauty. We were just commencing the ascent of the Alleghanny Mountains. My
friends will remember I crossed them going west between
Altoona & Pittsburgh en route for Ohio Y.M. but this route
the Baltimore & Ohio Railway is incomparably more lovely.
& oh! I did long to have my wife & all I most love to share
the scenery with me. The railroad winds along up-up-up,
now across some rocky glen with mountain torrents foaming
below, now in a deep cutting, or through a tunnel rough
hewn out of the rock, now across a long bridge of tressels.
About 9 we reached the top, & had breakfast at Grafton.
The mountain slopes are richly draped from base to summit
with trees of varied sort, all in their fullest Autumn glory,
like one enormous flower show, & under the trees in all
directions, the stag-horn'd shumach, all over brightest crim-
son. This is considered the finest railway journey in the
United States. Leaving Grafton, we wind down the eastern
slope, along the Cheet River valley, with its rocks & water-
falls, gloriously beautiful.[13] Then along the Potomac River,
broad & lovely, to Harpers Ferry, a place of intense loveli-
ness & immortalized as the place where John Brown built
his fort & was afterwards captured.[14] "His body lies mould-
ering in the grave, but his soul goes marching on." Here,
the Potomac is joined by a river Shenondoah rushing along
a narrow bed to join its bigger sister & flow into Chesapeak
Bay. Thence along the river side, we still travelled to the
Capital of the United States, Washington, where, by the
waning light of evening we could distinguish the noble

---

[13] Spelled "Cheat."

[14] John Brown seized the town briefly in 1859, but he did not hold it long
enough to build a fort.

dome of its Capitol. Then on to Baltimore, where at the depot, Dr. James Cary Thomas met us at 9 P.M. & drove us to his comfortable home where several Friends are lodging for Y.M. William Ladd & his daughter M. among the number. Supped & soon retired—weary, with about 1300 miles travelling, since 3rd day afternoon.

VII. Baltimore and North Carolina Yearly Meetings

7th day 10th mo: 20th Meeting on Ministry & Oversight at 10 o'clk. I was pleased to see C. Talbot & E. Comstock side by side, in the gallery. The former offered prayer, as did several others. E.C. & I preached. Then the opening Minute was read, & Minutes for the following Friends [:] W.R. from England, C.Talbot E.Comstock & Mary Elliot from Ohio, William Ladd & James Haviland from New York & Sarah J. Strang from Ohio. I was glad to see my kind friend & host on landing in Philadelphia, Dr. James Rhoads. He & several others from that isolated Y.M. are here, the distance not great.[1] Much counsel given & the reports read, & queries answered from the two Quarterly Meetings in Maryland & the half yearly meeting in Virginia, which together compose this very small Yearly Meeting, only contain in all about 500 members. The meetinghouse is nearly new & very commodious. It is a handsome building in a conspicuous part of the city. I dined at Deborah Thomas's. Her son Richard (who is Anna Lloyd Braithwaite's betrothed) & her daughter live with her.[2] A large party of Friends to dinner there. The Y. Meeting began at 4 o'clk. I opened it in prayer. Francis T. King is clerk. Friends gave me far too warm a welcome. It is a curious fact that the Alleghany Mountains seem to cut quakerism in two parts: *west*, they are all liberal in their actions as churches; *east* they are more like England—prudent, solemn & inclined to be conservative, no hymns sung,

---

[1] Philadelphia Yearly Meeting (Arch) was not in official correspondence with Baltimore, and thus the Philadelphia visitors, including ministers, were not carrying Minutes of introduction.

[2] Richard H. Thomas (1854–1904), actually a stepson of Deborah Thomas, was a physician. Anna Lloyd Braithwaite Thomas (1854–1947) was the daughter of J. Bevan Braithwaite, and the author of a number of volumes during her long and useful life. H-DQB.

friends rise during prayer, periods of silence are observed, & altogether after the five Western Y.M.'s I have attended, the change to the proprieties of Baltimore is quite curious. But they are a sweet choice body of intellectual & spiritual Friends, with whom it is a real priviledge to mingle. The heat is most oppressive here to day, I am again in a constant melt, indeed with only a very few cool days, I have been so ever since I landed, 9 weeks ago tomorrow. Routine business most of the sitting. Went to my home to tea where E. Comstock & others joined our party. In the evening was held a drawing-room meeting for all Friends who incline to come. It is regularly held on this evening during Y.M., a standing concern of my dear host & his lovely & excellent wife. It was largely attended, the drawing-room filled & a great many prayed & some gave their experience. Mary Thomas, E. Comstock & I spoke considerably. Broke up about 10 o'clk. To night is cooler & a heavy rain.

1st day 10th mo: 21st. A wet dull morning. Went to the Bible school—a nice lively time. Meeting for worship at 11 o'clk the meeting house very full. C. Talbot offered one of her very beautiful prayers. Then I spoke for nearly an hour. C.T. followed me & E.C. closed in prayer. James Carey drove me $3\frac{1}{2}$ miles to his home in the country, a very beautiful place among the hills & in view of Chesapeak Bay.[3] Called to see a rich Friend, an invalid with whom I prayed. After dinner back into Baltimore to the afternoon meeting which I opened with prayer & W. Ladd spoke most of the time. Mary Elliot adding a few words. Tea at my home & then to the evening meeting which Dr. J.C. Thomas opened with prayer. Then I spoke a long while. E.C. followed me. Deborah Thomas gave thanks & prayed very beautifully. M. Elliot spoke & C. Talbot closed in

---

[3] James Carey (1821–1894) spent his entire life in the Baltimore area. He studied at Haverford, married Susan B. Kimber, and was active in business and philanthropic work. *The Friend* (Phila.) **68** (1895): p. 120. H-DQB.

prayer.[4] We have had most blessed meetings to day. Spent a quiet hour of religious converse at our quarters, closing the day with singing hymns & prayer from dear Mary Thomas.

2nd day 22nd Baltimore is a noble city of 400.000 inhabitants & the parts I have yet visited are very substantial looking, rows of red brick mansion like houses with flights of polished white marble steps to the front doors giving a very aristocratic effect to the place. There are several Philadelphia Friends here. One a minister sat next to me at meeting yesterday (Samuel Balderson) is the principal minister of the north meeting, the narrowest in that city & to my great surprise, he requested me very earnestly to attend their meeting which I think I shall probably do. Devotional meeting at 8.30 A.M. I was requested to conduct it. Dr. Rhoads spoke most excellently & we had a very good meeting but so quiet & proper after those west of the Alleghanny. No groaning, or singing or responding. Y.M. at 10. Epistles read & other routine work. Dear Caroline Talbot & Mary Elliot visited our Men's meeting.[5] This journal leaves me in good health & thankful for our loving Father's many mercies.

2nd day 10th Mo: 22nd Devotional meeting again at 4 P.M. & in the evening a Home mission meeting—very interesting. Dr. Garner gave us a nice address. He is the man who is doing such great & good work in East Tenessee among the poor degraded white population. He says, 100.000 children in Tenessee, Carolina, Georgia & Allabama cannot read or write. He has instituted over 500 schools

[4] *Friends Review* reported that his morning sermon was from Isaiah 55: 6,7, "Seek, forsake, return"; and that in the evening his theme was, "What mean these stones?" **31** (1877): p. 187.

[5] Mary Elliott (1814?–1902) was born in east Tennessee, lived for some time in Kansas, and was blind for the last twelve years of her life. *American Friend* **9** (1902): p. 279.

among them.[6] Before the meeting closed, I gave the workers a short practical address.

3rd day 10th mo: 23rd Devotional meeting at which again Dr. Rhoads & I took the lead. He left for home to day. The "Friends Review," (of which he is editor & is issued weekly) occupies much of his time. During the morning sitting I paid a visit to the Women's meeting & felt much help & power there, got back again in time to speak to the Men on the state of the Society, also on the separation in Western Y.M. as they had received two Epistles from that body & did not know quite, how best to act. As I had seen the separation I could of course, give the facts of the case, greatly to the relief of some Friends, who wanted the meeting to address an Epistle to the separated Friends.[7] Dined at Francis T. King's. My friends will probably remember him (an Elder) at our Y.M. He has three very accomplished daughters. He is a widower. They live in a very beautiful home, in the very lap of luxury. I rejoice to find he means to go to North Carolina Y. M. Devotional meeting this afternoon, very excellent. I went to tea at Thomas Wilson's. He is a Friend 88 years old, able to walk alone & gave us, an excellent address this morning. He was only converted when he was 76. He is extremely wealthy & has willed his money to the founding of charitable institutes.[8] Met C. Talbot & E. Comstock there, to tea. At dinner today, I sat by Sarah Murray of N. York who was at our dear Aunt P. Green's 17 years ago & at the house of her parents our dear Aunt stayed 3 mos. After tea, was held at the meetinghouse a youth's meeting, at the appointment of C. Talbot & W. Robson but C.T. told me she only

[6] See note 16, Part II.

[7] This is slightly confusing. W.R. would have suggested that Baltimore Yearly Meeting not send an epistle to the separated group in Western Yearly Meeting, and it did not do so. *Minutes of Baltimore Yearly Meeting of Friends,* 1877: pp. 6, 11.

[8] Thomas Wilson (1789?–1879) left money both to Quaker programs and to several city projects. *Friends Review* 33 (1879): p. 89.

had her name added, to encourage me. She felt she had very little to say. It was a memorable meeting—so full that there was neither seat nor standing room for any more, & crowds outside the door, as it was advertised for the Youth of Baltimore, yet so quiet, one might almost hear a pin drop. C.T. soon offered one of her beautiful prayers, described by S.H. Lury, as "taking hold of the throne of Grace." Then I spoke for nearly an hour.[9] C.T. followed with a loving addition. E. Comstock followed with one of her thrilling addresses & anecdotes, & M. Elliot & Dr. Thomas closed in prayer. The dear young people seemed in no hurry to leave & were as attentive & earnest as ever it was my lot to preach to. This has been a day of great blessing to me & I am thankful to get another letter from my precious wife with good news of her & all my dear ones. A kind note from J. B. Braithwaite gives the account of the sudden death of Samuel Bewley (Dublin).[10] The clerk announced this from the desk in a tearful address.

4th day 24th Devotional meeting peculiarly favoured this morning—many most satisfactory testimonies given. At 10 we met in "joint session," men & women Friends to hear the London General Epistle read & various documents of interest discussed. After we adjourned, W. Ladd, his daughter & I ascended the Washington Monument, nearly 200 feet high to see the glorious view all over the city & its suburbs, & Chesapeek Bay, which in the unclouded sunshine looked lovely.[11] Descended & dined together at Joseph Elliot's. He is a wealthy man & lives in

[9] W.R. began "with the words, 'Remember now thy Creator in the days of thy youth,' and spoke at length with much power." *Friends Review* **31** (1877): p. 202. Samuel Harford Lury (1809–1892) was a member of W.R.'s home meeting in Saffron Walden. Born in Bristol, he was the author of two pamphlets on the atonement. L-DQB.

[10] Samuel Bewley (1806–1877) was clerk of Dublin Yearly Meeting for several years, and had twice visited America to travel in the ministry. He had a concern for temperance and for the Freedmen. L-DQB.

[11] Not to be confused with the monument in Washington, D.C.

style. His aged mother in law lives with them. Her name is
Sarah Janney widow of Richard Janney, a name well
known, I think, to us in England.[12] Devotional meeting
again this afternoon—very blessed. Home to tea & then
to meetinghouse where I gave a lecture on Mission work in
the Islands, largely attended & apparently appreciated.
Baltimore races & the election of Mayor have made a great
commotion here, all day.

5th day 10th mo 25th Devotional meeting as usual at
8.30. Closing meeting on Ministry & Oversight at 9.30.
A returning Minute prepared for J. B. Braithwaite, accord-
ing to a very peculiar custom. I am to have mine sent
me next year.[13] Meeting for worship at 11 o'clk, large &
very solemn. C. T. in prayer. Then I spoke with more
than usual of the conscious help of the Holy Spirit, on the
Divinity of Christ. C. T. & E. C. followed. Then M. Elliot
& W. R. in prayer & praise. Afterwards, I found there were
many Hicksites present, so we are led by Him in whose
sight all things are naked & open. Took a touching farewell of dear C. Talbot who I expect not to meet again
till we meet in Heaven. She gave me a holy kiss before
she left the gallery. I called on Esther Tuttle, a sweet
minister who has the care of a large school next to the
meetinghouse, owned by Friends. Her husband (Professor
Tuttle) is the Principal of it.[14] Dined at Rachel Brown's
a dear aged Friend of about 80. She told me of being at
a relations wedding 50 years ago, at which Ruth Ely &
Elizabeth Robson were present. Grandmother requested

[12] Richard M. Janney (1806?–1874) was born in Virginia, and was a lifelong
friend of the Negro, felt a deep concern for those in prison, and served as an
elder in his monthy meeting. His widow, Sarah (1800?–1879) was also an
elder, and had been confined to her bed for many years. *Friends Review* **28**
(1875): pp. 325, 329; **32** (1879): p. 745.

[13] Braithwaite had been at Baltimore in 1876, and thus under the practice
of waiting for a year before preparing a minute, his was drawn up in 1877.

[14] Lucius V. Tuttle had taken over as principal of the Friends Elementary
and High School in 1875. William C. Dunlap, *Quaker Education in Baltimore
and Virginia Yearly Meetings* . . . (Philadelphia, 1936), p. 55.

to have a meeting at the bride's house which was most unwillingly granted. At that meeting she prophesied of coming death & very few days afterwards, three of that party died. The closing sitting of the Y. M. was at 3.30. Epistles &c. read. Then Deborah Thomas sent a request that the men would join the women upstairs to close the meeting together. This was done, D. T. giving us a very earnest address & offered beautiful prayer. I spoke a few closing words & then the men's clerk read his & the womens clerk her closing Minutes & Baltimore Y. M. was over. F. T. King met all of us who are bound to N. Carolina in a solemn conclave—then another committee & then home to tea where by accident I found I was sitting by the side of a cousin of my brother Arthur Midgley, a woman friend, maiden name Alice Fothergill, now Tatham, a 4th wife I think. At 8 o'clk a meeting assembled in our host's drawingroom of some 50 or 60 Friends to consecrate their service to the Lord for Home mission work. I addressed & prayed with them. Several spoke & prayed. John B. Crenshaw of Richmond prayed fervently for me, my work, my dear wife, & my little ones.[15] Broke up at 10 o'clk. I feel I have cause to ask the prayers of my friends at home that my blessed Master will keep me very humble, for I never knew anything like the love & unity heaped on me here, even by Philadelphia Friends, & several have publicly confessed to great spiritual blessings from my service. I can & do most surely feel & know it is the Lord's work & not mine, but praised be His name, He has wonderfully owned & blessed me the last few weeks—more than ever before.

6th day 26th After an early breakfast, my kind friend

[15] John B. Crenshaw (1820–1889) a life long Virginian, studied at Haverford, and was recorded as a minister in 1854. He actively aided conscientious objectors in the south during the Civil War, visited the wounded, and helped Freedman. He edited the *Southern Friend* for two years. *Quaker Biog.*, ser. II, 3: p. 165. H-DQB.

W. Ladd & his daughter Marianna took me with them to spend a few hours at Washington, the capital of the United States, an hour's ride of 40 miles from Baltimore. James Underhill, who resides there, & has been at Y. M. here, kindly acted as our guide. Went first to the treasury & saw every process of printing, preparing & issuing bank-notes (Green-backs) of every value from 1 dollar to 100. Women are very largely used for this work. As we were leaving we saw a real American sight—Barnium's great procession reaching nearly a mile of all the strange & curious things that could easily be imagined.[16] Then to the "White House" where we were ushered into a very grandly furnished & spacious reception room, & a gentleman kindly took us into three private drawingrooms, all very splendid, the Blue, Green & Red rooms. Soon a message came that the President was ready to see us, & we were politely ushered into the presence of Hayes the President of the United States. He is a very fine noble looking man, he shook hands with us all & on hearing who I was, he said, "Mr. Robson I am delighted to see you." He had a little chat with us about Friends, but so many senators were waiting to see him that we could not stay many minutes. I thought of my late dear Aunt & her visit to President Buchanan.[17] Thence to the Capitol—the great Senate & Representative house of the United States. I had no idea of its being such a magnificent place. The dome is 335 feet high & very elegant, surmounted by a very large bronze image of an Indian chief. The interior is arranged & furnished regardless of cost—polished marble walls & pillars. At one end is the Senate house, the other,

[16] P. T. Barnum (1810–1891) was the great showman of his day, and formed his circus, "the Greatest Show on Earth" in 1871. *DAB.*

[17] Rutherford B. Hayes (1822–1893) had taken office earlier in 1877. Friends were actively engaged in discussions with him about the Indian question at this time. *DAB.* Priscilla Green had seen President James Buchanan (1791–1868) during her visit mentioned earlier.

the Representative house. Near the centre is the supreme court where we saw the chief justice trying a civil suit. Ascended the Dome to the whispering Gallery, very similar in size & effect to St. Pauls London. Outside, on the top of the Dome, is a grand view all round. The city is not built "4 square" like most American cities, but the Capitol is the centre & the streets all diverge from it. Dined in the refreshment room of the Capitol. Returned to tea, which I partook of at Deborah Thomas's. Then to the meetinghouse where I had appointed a meeting, wishing also that good old Samuel Balderson from Philadelphia, who has sat by me all the Y. M. should have an opportunity to speak. After I had prayed, he spoke $\frac{1}{2}$ an hour & a more perfect hash of Wilburism I never heard. The seed of God in the heart was the topic continually referred to. I felt it very sad & had I had the least idea of his views would never have asked him to join me in the meeting, but he always seemed so full of unity with me that I fancied him all right. I spoke as clearly as I ever was enabled to, on the offices of Christ, His blood &c, knowing that Hicksites were present in numbers. Dr. J. C. Thomas closed in prayer & praise. Then it seemed as if all Baltimore Friends must have a few last words with me & it was after 10 when I left the house. Francis R. King kindly escorted me home.

7th day 10th mo 27th It is difficult to realize that here in Baltimore, before the civil war a few years ago, only 12 I believe, almost everybody but Friends held slaves & bought & sold them, but Dr. Thomas has told me things that he has met with in his medical experience that fully confirm the worst statements in H. B. Stowe's "Uncle Tom." After breakfast W. Ladd & Marianna left for their home at Brooklyn, N. York. The Doctor drove me into the city to visit the John Hopkins university. J. H. was a Friend who made his money by grocery & left 2½ million dollars, chiefly to Friends as Trustees, for a University & I presume there are few establishments in the world more replete with every comfort & everything for its efficiency.[18] Then we visited the Bank for safe deposit, also the Young Men's Christian Association. Then packed up, after which Dr. Thomas drove me through the Park, one of the loveliest in America, most of the original forest left, in hill & dale, deep gorges & rocky heights. Art only being used to make good roads, plant young trees & make dams for water supply &c. Dinner, & then took leave of the choice friends who have been so kind & loving to me & left Baltimore at 3.15. An hour to wait in Washington gave me the chance of a hasty run up to the Capitol. Then on to Richmond, Virginia where I am located at the house of W. H. Pleasance, reaching here at 11.30. P.M.[19]

1st day 10th mo: 28th After reading, W. P. took me a walk to the brow of a high hill to overlook the city. Richmond has a population of 75000—it is an old colonial place & its people have much of the old English aristocratic feeling about them. It was the fall of this city which closed the civil war 12 years ago. Was driven to meeting 2 miles away—the house pretty well filled. I felt it hard work to preach, as if I was combating error & found after meeting that some very strong Hicksites were present, but I was wonderfully favored. John B. Crenshaw, their [i.e., the Orthodox] only Minister extended a special invitation to the afternoon meeting when we broke up. Dined at Jane Whitlaw's. At her house Friends held their meetings during the war amid the roar of cannon & here J. J. Neave used to meet with them & very lovingly they held him in remembrance.[20] Their afternoon meeting was large & very

---

[18] Johns Hopkins (1795–1873) was in several other business enterprises, and was the largest stockholder in the Baltimore and Ohio Railroad. *DAB.*

[19] The family name is "Pleasants."

[20] Jane Copeland Whitlock (1806?–1888) was an elder in Richmond Monthly Meeting for forty years. *Friends Review* **42** (1888): p. 159.

solemn. J. B. Crenshaw drove me home with him afterwards. He lives 5 miles away from Richmond at a very
pretty farm. He is a man well known to all who studied
the position of Southern Friends during the war. He did
more than anyone else for the poor soldiers, wounded &
dying & for the Friends who were imprisoned & tortured
for refusing to fight. Passed the house of the rebel President
Jefferson Davis.[21] He now lives in the state of Mississippi.

2nd day 10.29 After an early breakfast, J. B. Crenshaw
drove me into Town & to the grounds, where is to be held
tomorrow a great Agricultural show for the state of Virginia
—he is exhibiting Steam thrashing & other machines. Now
I must close this, as I want to post it before going on further
South this afternoon. I go, D. V. to the Black Creek tonight,
where a meeting is fixed for me tomorrow morning,[22] thence
on to Somerton to a meeting in the evening & on to New
Garden where N. Carolina Y. M. is held, on 4th day. A
man Friend of Richmond, Boling Whinston accompanies
me to Black Creek tonight.[23] I am still blessed with good
health & look back with very deep thankfulness to the six
Y. M.'s I have attended on this great Continent & especially
I feel I did right in going West a second time to be at
Kansas Yearly Meeting after I had given it up. I feel sure
I was in my right place there. Now I have only one more
Y. M. to attend & I know not what may await me there,
not much of the good things of this life I am well assured,
but I have firm faith that He who has in great mercy
equipped me for six Y. Meetings, will also qualify me for
the seventh, & then I have only N. York & Brooklyn &
finally Philadelphia & then to my dear home! Pray for

[21] Jefferson Davis (1808–1889) headed the Confederate government located
in Richmond during the war. *DAB.*
[22] "D.V." God willing.
[23] Bowling H. Winston (1823?–1892) was born in Virginia and studied at
the University of Virginia. He spent a number of years in Indiana, and then
returned to his native state in 1871. *Friends Review* 45 (1892): p. 669.

me that I may be kept always close to Christ Jesus, neither lifted up, nor cast down. It is a blessed experience, "Great peace have they that love Thy law, & nothing shall offend them."

2nd day 10th Mo: 29th Wrote home letters at John B. Crenshaw's office till nearly time to leave Richmond. Boling Whinston joined me at the depot & we travelled together to Ivor where we found a carriage & pair of horses waiting to convey us to our quarters for the night. A drive of nearly twenty miles through the forest was a great treat, though the land is too poor to produce big trees. Pines are the principal growth. After it was quite dark, we arrived at the very comfortable home of Denson & Mary Pretlow. After driving miles over a corderoy road with swamps all round, it was very cheering to be ushered into a fine parlour with a blazing log fire & a warm welcome from all the family. We bowed in prayer & praise together before retiring for the night.

3rd day 10th mo: 30th On looking out of my window this morning, I see we are in a cotton plantation. This reminds one of the days of Virginian slavery & perhaps one gets rather the brighter view of that awful blot on civilization in this comfortable place, from the fact that the black servants & field hands about us, were slaves born & reared as such, on this very spot, but so kindly treated that they stay with their master now, by choice. Denson Pretlaw is not a Friend, his wife is, & he more of one than any other profession. I had as black a little "nigger" boy as ever I saw, come rushing into my room this morning for my boots & to bring me water—a civil little fellow—a sort of boy would be very handy as "a Tiger" at home.[24] After breakfast, I was driven 5 miles to Black Creek meeting-house, away in the primeval forest, no house near it, but found about 120 Friends & others who have come from

[24] A "tiger" was a smartly liveried boy acting as a groom or footman.

various distances of from one to ten miles to hear the English Friend. These specially appointed meetings are a very great exercise to my mind. One feels one ought to have something very powerful to preach to dear people coming so far to hear one. But my God has always been much better to me than my fears, & we had a very blessed time. My kind companion Boling Winston opened in prayer, & after I had spoken for about an hour, a young friend Sallie Harris prayed & I closed in praise & prayer. S. Harris drove me to her father's to dine. He is Matthew Harris, an aged invalid. Then Oswin White drove me, & B. Winston drove his sister Deborah Pretlaw twenty long miles over a horrible road (swampy & corderoy) to Somerton. We were more than 4 hours on the journey & passed on the way the Blackwater River which was the boundary line between the two forces during the civil war. Various burnt buildings & earth trenches speak of the horrid conflict. Arrived at William H. Hare's about 6.30. He is a good man who was shot & left for dead by a Southern Officer in the war, because he acted as a Christian.[25] His wife Ann Hare is a minister. After tea groped our dark way to the Meeting, wading two streams, but got safely to the House, & to our surprise found nearly 100 people assembled & we had a good time. Boling Winston has kindly fixed to go on with me to N. Carolina, which we hope to reach tomorrow night. We are now almost close to the "Dismal Swamp." [26]

4th day 10th Mo: 31st After an early breakfast, we were driven 8 miles to the Depot, where after an hour's wait, we "got aboard the cars" for Raleigh the capital of North

[25] William H. Hare (1816?–1894) was an elder in the Somerton meeting, and his wife Ann (1821–1881) a minister. The *Friend* (Phila.) **68** (1895): p. 152; *Friends Review* **34** (1881): p. 649.

[26] Named by William Byrd in 1728, and covering 750 square miles, Dismal Swamp had been made famous by Longfellow's poem, "The Slave in the Dismal Swamp."

Carolina which we reached about 5.30 P.M. & hoped to get on to New Garden, but find the only train in the day from here to that neighbourhood, leaves here at 2 o'clk tomorrow morning, so feeling very weary & myself almost broken down, we took a bedroom at Osborne House, a very 3d. rate Hotel, & intend to retire very early to get a few hours sleep before any more rushing over the country.

[5th day, 11th mo 1st] Rose, not much refreshed at about ½ an hour after midnight & repaired to the depot. The cars came at 2 A.M. & we reached Greensboro at 8. There we breakfasted & at 9.30. took the cars on to New Garden only 7 miles further & the only train in the day. Met by several Friends at New Garden. This is a curious & very picturesque place for a Yearly Meeting. It is just a cleared patch in the forest of oaks & pines which extends miles & miles in every direction. The principal buildings are the meetinghouse, a very nice & nearly new one, & the great Friends boarding school where nearly all the Y.

FIG. 6. North Carolina Friends gathered at New Garden for yearly meeting. (Drawing by John Collins, 1869.)

Meeting are fed & lodged—three in a bed often, for none are refused. Through the very kind thoughtfulness of J. B. Braithwaite, who knows that we Englishmen do not like sleeping three in a bed, I am housed at Jonathan Cox's ¼ of a mile from meeting where I am favored with a room to myself of which I am exceedingly thankful, for I am very weary, bodily, spiritually & mentally. He has some nice Friends lodging here, among others the Fletchers whose daughter Elma Coffin was one of my kind escorts to Spiceland. The Y. M. met at 10 o'clk. I was there by 11, just in time to present my certificates in due course. The Select Y. M. was yesterday—the day altered this year of which fact no one here, informed me. The meeting occupied with Epistles & preliminaries generally.[27] Glad once more to meet Sarah Satterthwaite (who I last saw in Ohio). E. Comstock, Julia Valentine & several who were at Baltimore are also here. We had a nice meeting for worship in the afternoon. I was permitted to give the "keynote." "Jesus Christ & Him crucified." [28] One strong Wilbur Friend spoke in opposition, but prevailed nothing. It is a real pleasure to me to renew the acquaintance of dear Allen Jay who is now a member of N. Carolina Y. M. Abraham Fisher (Jane Wright's brother) who my friends will remember, is a very active member here.[29] He asked after my relations & other Walden Friends.

[27] The list of visiting ministers included the three English Friends, Sarah B. Satterthwaite, Hannah Thistlethwaite, and W. R.; James M. Haviland and Ruth S. Murray of New York; Elizabeth Comstock and Sarah Jane Strang of Ohio; Julia Valentine from Baltimore; William West and Mary P. Moon of Indiana; and Louisa Painter of Iowa. Six additional visiting ministers were noted later: Rufus P. King, Pheribe Toms, and Elizabeth and Josiah White from Indiana; and Daniel Martin and Elam Jessup from Iowa. A number of the ministers were accompanied by companions, and it was obvious that the other yearly meetings were concerned to support North Carolina Friends by sharing in these sessions. *Minutes of North Carolina Yearly Meeting of Friends*, 1877: pp. 4, 6.

[28] *Friends Review* reported that he used the text, "One thing I know, whereas I was blind, now I see," and "stressed salvation through the blood of Christ." 31 (1877): p. 218.

[29] Abraham Fisher (1823–1909) was born in Ireland, and after a time in

6th day 11th mo: 2nd After early breakfast, I went to the schoolhouse to call on some of the dear Friends who are housed there. Dear Rufus King arrived last night. He seems well, but deeply feels the death of his dear Mother. He says he believes he was at Illawarra Cottage the very hour I was at his mother's funeral.[30] He never thought he should not see her alive, till one day on board the ship, he felt he could not pray for her, & then he felt quite sure, she was past the need of his prayers, yet he said when he was met with the news of her death, it almost broke his heart. Meeting on M. & Oversight at 9—an interesting meeting much occupied in the consideration of some unsoundness in the ministry in some meetings, Hicksite views showing themselves. In the Y. M. we had the state of the Society, on which R. K. Allen Jay & W. R. were the chief speakers. We had a long sermon also from a man on the great principle of wearing coats unlike the world! I presume he edified himself, but surely not the Church. I have a sweet letter today from dear Hannah W. Smith to arrange my visit to them in Philadelphia. After dinner went to meeting again, held for discussing the work done by this Y. Meeting. I would have liked all my dear ones to have been present to hear all the efforts of these dear Friends in setting up meetings [,] establishing schools & preaching the Gospel of Jesus Christ. It is wonderful when we consider how this Y. Meeting was almost ruined by the curse of slavery, & decimated by the Civil war— Friends robbed of all they possessed & yet in this State, in Tenesee, Alabama & Georgia, they are labouring among the poor Whites, 51 per cent of whom cannot read or write, also among the coloured freedmen & the Indians. Dr. Garner has 2000 of the latter under his sole care. All

England, returned there where he married Sarah Wright. He had reached North Carolina in 1874 after a time in South America. H-DQB.

[30] "Illawarra Cottage" was the name W. R. and his wife had given their home in Saffron Walden.

they want is means. I almost long to be rich that I might give them substantial help in their work. H. Thistlethwaite, her sister,[31] E. Comstock & I gave them short addresses & I prayed for them. Home to our quarters & to bed about ½ after 9 o'clk, two meals a day, breakfast & dinner being the rule here. This is a rustic locality, all among the Oak trees, one wonders how first a settlement was made here. The wells in this part of the State remind me of the dear old well in Dr. Cox's lovely home at Summerhill. They all work on the same principle with a long lever & a chain.

7th day 11th mo: 3rd. Meeting on Ministry & Oversight again this morning. I requested & was granted an opportunity to address the members of that meeting on many very important points of doctrine & practice. The Y. M. met with open shutters in joint session at 11. Passed several reports of Indian work education &c. A dear Minister of Tennesee, Rachel Binford, was very cordially liberated to visit England & Ireland. She is a wonderful woman, who has been the means of establishing not only several Particular meetings, but one Quarterly & several Monthly Meetings, a woman of (probably) nearly 50 years of age. I believe she will be welcomed at home. Allen Jay asked me to join the great throng of Friends at the school to dinner, which I did & much enjoyed it. After that meal was over, I was asked up into one of the bedrooms where we met men & women ministers & had much interesting converse & some very amusing anecdotes from Allen Jay & Rufus King. Then Julia Valentine (old Dr. Thomas's sister) asked me into her bedroom where 8 women Friends sleep in four beds. Here was a scene for more like old Boarding-school days, if the dear friends had all been about 16 years old instead of from 40 to 70. One brought out a teapot & cooked some tea, another produced some roast

---

[31] He means her sister-in-law, Sarah Satterthwaite.

chestnuts, another some biscuits & a fourth some apples, & we all had a feast. J. Valentine, Ruth Murray, Rachel Binford, Allen Jay, E. Comstock & W. R. all ministers & Sarah Murray & two others, elders. This is one of the time honoured institutions of N. Carolina Y. Meeting. Evening meeting was on 1st day schools, very interesting, especially dear Rufus's experience. He made all the meeting cry this morning as he gave us his awful experiences in the battle of Gettesburg, among the wounded & dying. Closed by a Devotional meeting conducted by Rufus & me. I close this to night because tomorrow will be a full day, & I go tomorrow evening to Greensboro to have a meeting there & shall not probably return till next morning. This leaves me well & very thankful for the help graciously afforded, weary but able to work.

7th day 11th mo: 3rd It is a curious sight at the close of an evening meeting to see all round the meetinghouse at little distances, in the darkness, the bright glare of the camp fires telling of families of Friends attending Y. Meeting, too poor to board at the school where they only charge a dollar a day & night for each person, but these poor Friends bring the food with them in their waggons & in these they sleep & live when not in meeting.

1st day 4th. Meeting at 8.30. I suppose 500 or more assembled, & several spoke. I did for nearly ½ an hour, Abraham Fisher at some length, Ruth Murray &c.[32] Broke up at 10.30 & the shutters were (at my request) removed so as to lay all the house into one. Outside was a curious sight—vehicles of all sorts drawn by horses, mules & donkeys & *one* by a very fine Ox, filled the space all round the house, as thousands of people poured in, some by special trains, but many in their own conveyances. At

[32] Ruth Murray was the widow of Robert Lindley Murray, clerk of New York Yearly Meeting when he died suddenly in 1874. She moved to New Bedford, Mass., in 1879. Hinshaw, *Encyclopedia of American Quaker Genealogy* **3**: p. 239.

11 o'clk began the meetings—one outside & the house crowded. It is estimated to hold nearly two thousand & it was very full to day & extra seats brought in. In the galleries were a motley group of Black people, the men with their woolly heads, the negresses with jaunty looking hats & dresses of the gayest conceivable colours. Dear old Julia Valentine offered a long & beautiful prayer & then I rose & preached for 1 & ¼ hours, with more than usual power—a great & special blessing at such a time. Jeremiah Grenel closed in prayer. I went out to the preaching stand where Rufus was still preaching. Home to my quarters to dine & then back to meeting at 2 o'clk. Rufus indoors, Ruth Murray & I at the stand. A great crowd gathered round, as dear R. M. read & prayed then I spoke for an hour & R. M. followed briefly, the people both morning & afternoon as quiet & attentive all the times as I ever wish to address. Dr. Benbow of Greensboro' then took Allen Jay & me in his carriage to his home at Greensboro' the county town, a place of about 4000 persons.[33] After tea we went to the Methodist chapel, where I preached to a large & interesting congregation, greatly increased by about 200 young women & girls from a College nearby. A. Jay closed the service in prayer & we returned to Dr. Benbows. He is a Friend who has not practiced as a Physician for many years, but lives at & owns a very fine Hotel called Benbow House. The other Hotel keepers in Greensboro' now allow him a good income annually to keep his Hotel closed, so he lives in it as a private house with 70 rooms & we had our meals in a room with accomodation for 100 to dine easily, set out with tables. It is all well furnished & very comfortable. Four sermons a day. Two very long ones to very large congregations sent me to bed weary & hoarse, but very thankful for the rich blessings of to day.

[33] Dr. D. W. C. Benbow (1830?–1902). *American Friend* **9** (1902): p. 744.

2nd day 11th mo: 5th. After an early breakfast, drove into New Garden with the Dr. & his wife. A soaking rain to day makes the roads impassable but we got safely in at 9.15. to the meeting on Ministry & Oversight. The Y. M. at 11. I was liberated to visit the Women's meeting & spoke to the dear sisters till tears flowed plentifully. One poor woman fell on the floor fainting, & was carried out, but it did not hinder us long. When I returned into the Men's house, I found a Methodist minister preaching. He came as a deputation from that body & when he had done, he too, was liberated to visit the Women which he did, A. Jay with him. Passing Reports &c. this morning. One Monthly Meeting that of Deep Creek has 150 members forming two Preparative Meetings who are in this state. They have no Friends with education enough to transact the business of the meeting, or able to read the Minutes of travelling ministers. This gives a little idea of how things are in North Carolina Y. Meeting. After dinner I gave the Friends my South Sea Island lecture, which the dear simple hearted people listened to with wonderful interest, as if they had never heard of such people or places before. Went to the School House & had tea again in J. Valentines & Co's bedroom & some very interesting conversation with the dear sisters there. John Thomas there also. In the evening, Mission & Temperance work, principally addressed by A. Jay, Dr. Garner & E. Comstock. This day eight years has been much before my mind all day, when in Sydney I took my beloved Christina to be my dear wife. Truly I bless the Lord for the precious gift He conferred upon me then.

3rd day 11th mo: 6th At 9 this morning a Youth's meeting was held at the request of Ruth Murray & myself & proved a very large & deeply interesting meeting & many dear young hearts were deeply touched & many tears were shed.[34] Broke up 11. at which hour began the closing sitting of the Y. Meeting. After passing several Reports, we received Revd. Nathan Hunt Wilson D. D. deputation from the Methodist Episcopal Church who gave us a very sweet address & afterwards visited the Women. Then dear E. Comstock & S. Satterthwaite paid our meeting a favoured visit. Rufus King visited the Women's meeting. Then returning Minutes were read & a very cordial one given to me. Then all the Epistles were read & the Minute of advice & one also from the Meeting of Oversight & Ministry. After this, dear old Julia Valentine paid us a very solemn visit, saying she felt she would never be at this Y. Meeting again. After she left, I gave a farewell address dear Rufus prayed earnestly for my dear ones & for safe voyaging for me & I returned praise & thanksgiving for the mercies of our dear God in Christ Jesus. The Clerk, Isham Cox read the closing Minute & N. Carolina Y. Meeting was at an end.[35] It was 4.30 when we came away & certainly after sitting from 9 till 4.30 were ready for some food for our bodies, having had our souls fed very graciously. Thus has closed the seventh & last Y. M. I was liberated to attend, & I feel I must record the deep gratitude I feel for the wonderful help granted me by my gracious Lord. I have gone to each of these Meetings feeling very empty but power has always been given when I needed it & I have not shunned to declare all the counsel of God as He has made it known to me. I *do* give *him* all the praise. After a late dinner, I wrote the above in the dim twilight, & then went to the school, to take a general farewell of the Friends there. Rufus & I have been very closely knit together & I feel deeply for him. Finding his

---

[34] "A time of blessing from the Lord," said *Friends Review* **31** (1877): p. 233.

[35] Isham Cox (d. 1894) was a minister, and had been very active in defending conscientious objectors in North Carolina during the Civil War. H-DQB.

Mother dead, he has sold his furniture & home at Spiceland & is now homeless, but I believe has a home in the
hearts of many of the Lord's people. Had a last cup of tea
in Julia Valentine's room where a number of choice Friends
assembled & we had a nice parting time. Professor Hartley
& his wife (the Principals of the School) Ruth Murray, S.
Satterthwaite & her sister &c. there.[36] Then back to Jonathan Cox's & was driven in his carriage to the depot 1½
mile off. It was a very dark night & bad road. On reaching
the depot which has no house, only a platform, a number
of Friends like myself waiting for the train, had kindled
a large bonfire & we stood round it telling experiences of
life &c. till the cars came up. At Greensboro' I took a
Pulman or Lucas sleeper & had a good night, it being cool
& only a few people in the car.

[36] George N. Hartley (1844–1938) was born in Ohio, and moved out to Iowa
before returning to Indiana to study at Earlham. He went to New Garden in
1871 and served the boarding school for a number of years. Dorothy Gilbert
(Thorne) *Guilford a Quaker College* (Greensboro, N.C., 1937). H-DQB.

VIII. New York, Niagara Falls, and Philadelphia

4th day 11th mo: 7. Reached Richmond, Virginia to breakfast, crossing James river which is wide & picturesque, foaming over great rocks. Then on Northward till we got to the great Potomac, along whose lovely banks we rode for many miles, till we reached Washington about 2 o'clk, & then on again (no time for food) as far as Baltimore, just a minute to buy an apple & then on again to Wilmington, Delaware where 20 minutes for supper was granted. Then on past Philadelphia & finally stopped at Jersey city N. York at 10. P.M. Here, William H. Ladd met me & we crossed the water which divides the main land from Long Island, in the steam ferry & landed at Brooklyn, whence 3 miles in a horse car brought us to his hospitable abode about 11.30. Marianna was up to welcome us & give me a letter from my dearest Tenie. Retired about midnight, very weary with travel.

5th day 11th mo. 8th Spent a quiet morning in conversation with W. & Caroline Ladd, the latter a sister of Charles T. Coffin. Their married daughter & her husband & two little ones live with them. After dinner, W. Ladd took me into New York, where we ascended Trinity Church spire, to a great & dizzy height in order to give me a good idea of this interesting locality. The city of New York contains one million inhabitants. It stands on an island (Manhattan by name) divided by the Hudson River from the main land where is Jersey city. The opposite side of N. York is divided by East River from Long Island on which stands Brooklyn with half a million souls. A vast quantity of shipping goes on in the two rivers which join & flow together into the Atlantic nearby. Visited the Post Office which is very grand. In Brooklyn we passed the ruins of the Theatre

which my friends will remember was burnt down last
Winter & some 130 lives lost.[1] Crossed from New York
to Brooklyn in a steam ferry boat containing about 1200
persons & 6 or 8 waggons & pairs of horses. About 100000
persons cross daily. After tea, W. Ladd, Marianna & I
went to a mission room in a low part of Brooklyn where
a young minister from Ohio is holding a course of services.
Her name is Lida G. Romick.[2] I spoke for half an hour.
Wondrous blessing from the Lord followed, many rose to
ask for prayer & gave themselves to the Lord. I did not
know of these services when I came here, but I feel more
than rewarded for coming here if only to attend a few
of them. Came home in a drenching rain.

6th day 11th Mo: 9th Marianna Ladd accompanied me
to her uncle Thomas Ladd's to breakfast. He is a very
earnest active minister. I was with him at Ohio Y. Meeting.
Then I paid a deeply interesting visit to Grace Dickenson
who was in England with Sarah Smiley & is herself an
Englishwoman.[3] Had much converse with her about her
late brother Abraham Davy & his family, & then went very
deeply into the subject of the baptism of the Holy Ghost.
She is a very favoured & advanced minister. I post this
to day so must draw to a close. Probably I may only send
one more journal, unless posting one just before sailing. I
intend to leave here for Niagara on 2nd day. It is a long
journey, but every one seems agreed I ought not to leave
America without seeing one of our Heavenly Father's most
glorious works in nature. It is a day's journey & I hope to
spend 3rd day there & reach Philadelphia on 4th day eve-

[1] The Brooklyn theater fire, on December 7, 1876, actually took nearly 300
lives. *Nation* **23** (1876): p. 349.

[2] Lida G. Romick served in many places during her lifetime. She spent
several years in Oregon in the 1890's, then after another period in Ohio, moved
to California where she died in 1912. *Ohio Yearly Meeting Minutes*, 1912:
p. 10.

[3] Grace Dickinson (d. 1886) was the wife of the minister, Henry Dickinson.
She accompanied Sarah Smiley (1830–1918) on a visit in the ministry to Britain
in 1869. *Friends Review* **39** (1886): p. 826.

ning & take up my abode at John B. Garretts as Dr.
Rhoads is not at home till 7th day, & then go to R. P.
Smith's to stay till I sail. H. W. S. has written to say she
has fixed a drawingroom meeting for me on 7th day evening. This leaves me well in body & rested mentally &
looking forward very brightly to a speedy reunion with all
I love best on earth. As the time draws nearer the tempta-
tion to impatience increases. We had a blessed prayer &
praise meeting after reading, Lida Romick being one of
our party.

6th day 11th mo 9th After dinner, W. Ladd took me in
a buggy a lovely drive to Brooklyn Park. This is new but
well laid out & many of the old forest trees still stand.
On a clear space in the highest part of the park we pulled
up to enjoy the grand view. Far off lay the Atlantic Ocean,
(my road home) & nearer, a pretty variety of fresh water
& land wooded, hilly. Long Island is 40 miles broad &
140 long. Drove from there to Green Wood Cemetery,
the finest in the United States & probably in the world.
I never saw half such a profusion of rich marble tombs
& mausoleums. Money is lavished by the living on the
dead in a wonderful way. Went in the evening again to
the Mission Meeting where Lida Romick & I had most
of the service & a nice after meeting &c.

7th day 10th A wet dismal day. W. Ladd took me across
to New York where we went over Stewart's great Drapery
Shop, the largest in the world. The late owner (of whom
we have often heard in England) began life as a common
Pedlar & at his death, his will was proved at eighty million
dollars (16 million pounds). It is a very grand establishment
occupying a whole block, facing 4 principal streets. Had
lunch & then paid a very interesting visit to the American
Bible House, where we saw every process of Bible making,
from the type setting to the binding & putting on gilt edges.
At tea, we were joined by Henry & Grace Dickenson &

Mary Johnson. The latter was at our Y. Meeting in London not long ago, as a Temperance advocate, at the Duchess of Sutherland's &c. She is a sister of Caroline Ladd's. Had an evening of deeply interesting religious conversation.

1st day 11.11. Accompanied W. Ladd & his daughter to the Bible School & then into the Meeting House. Special notice had been given in the papers, & the result was that Brooklyn Meeting House was well filled with a very solemn attentive congregation. Henry Dickenson offered prayer & then I spoke for over an hour on the words, "This is my beloved Son, hear Him." Rarely has it been my privilege to feel so much power & as I sat down, a dear minister called out, "Amen! bless the Lord." After I had prayed, H. Dickenson rose & gave the meeting a little account of me, which perhaps, interested the congregation, but I did not think added much to the edification of the meeting. Dined at Henry & Grace Dickenson's & received a call there from a good old Friend who is in deep trouble, having put his name to some documents he did not understand & is now out on bail, charged with perjury. W. Ladd called on me & we crossed to New York & took tea at William Thurston's. His wife was a daughter of Mahlon Day, who with *his* wife & daughter were drowned on their homeward voyage on the "Arctic." Here, I had the great pleasure of meeting Rebecca Collins who was very warm & insists that she well remembers me.[4] A meeting had been duly advertized for me at the great meetinghouse where New York Y. M. is held & we had a large attendance. I opened in prayer & then spoke a very long while. The people were very attentive, but yet it seemed wonderfully hard work. I perspired freely, not from bodily but spiritual exercise. A young minister offered a short prayer & then Grace

---

[4] Rebecca (Singer) Collins (*ca.* 1805–1892) was born in Philadelphia, and married Isaac Collins in 1835. She was a recorded minister, and visited England in 1866. H-DQB.

Dickenson a very sweet & rather long prayer & praise. When we broke up, I found that many there were Hicksites & some watching for anything they could object to, but Friends were very loving & pressed me to prolong my stay. Lulu Allen, (an old fellow passenger in the "Pensylvania" who I saw at Indianapolis) was there & came to speak to me. Reached my home at Brooklyn at 10.30.

2nd day 12th Spent quietly with my kind friends here, including a long walk with W. Ladd in the afternoon. Wrote many letters, read & discussed many very solemn doctrines, had some hymns in the evening & packed up, ready to depart on the morrow. My heart has felt specially drawn to these dear friends. They have had some sore trials, but are living earnest Christians.

3rd day 11th Mo: 13th After reading this morning, we had a very touching time in prayer, I praying for each occupant of the sweet home I was leaving & then my kind host for me, that I might leave a rich blessing & also take one with me & have a joyous meeting with all my loved ones at home. Then said farewell to my friends, to whom I feel to owe a debt of gratitude & W. Ladd escorted me to New York where he left me at the depot. Now began one of the finest rides I have ever been. Very soon after leaving N. York, we come to the right bank of the Hudson River & follow it for (I suppose) nearly 200 miles. The day was splendidly fine & cloudless, the river a brilliant blue & dotted over with pretty white sailing vessels & some steamboats. The opposite bank is very high, composed of almost perpendicular grey rocks, crowned with trees. This part is called the Pallisades. Further on, we pass almost close to the range of Catskill Mountains, grassy & pretty, but not wooded. Lunch at Poughkeepsie & then on to Albany where we crossed the Hudson over a fine iron bridge & turned westward up the valley of the Mohawk, which we followed till the sun had set & the moon-

light shone on the river at our feet. The Mohawk is not
so pretty as the Hudson, the banks being lower. Changed
trains at Rochester & reached Suspension Bridge station
at 1.15 A.M. on 4th day 11th Mo: 14th.

Lodged at an Hotel close to the depot & went to sleep
listening to the solemn roar of the great Waterfall two
miles away & felt " 'Tis the voice of the great Creator—
Dwells in that mighty tone." After I had breakfasted, set
off on foot along the path close to the side of the Niagara
River. All the way I could see ahead of me a pure white
cloud hanging like a veil over the glorious rush of waters,
the eternal cloud of spray which I presume has hung there,
perpetually changing, since God created this beautiful
earth. At my feet rushed the river, its course a very bois-
terous one, over rocks & fallen timber, forming the "Whirlpool Rapids." Two miles brought me to the town called
Niagara Falls & here, wishing to economise time & need-
ing a guide, I bargained with a flydriver to take me to all
the chief points of interest. First we crossed the flood of
waters on a wide suspension bridge, only recently finished,
the longest span in the world—1300 feet long & 190 feet
above the water, which is itself 184 feet in depth under
the bridge. From this giddy elevation, only wide enough
for one carriage & closed in windy weather, we get a
grand view of the falls. First, are two pretty little falls,
called the Bridal veil which would repay a visit if they
were all the attraction. Then comes the great American
Fall 460 feet wide & 170 feet high. Then Goat Island
covered with trees, projects out & cuts the river in two.
Then the great Canadian Falls or the Horseshoe fall 164
feet high & 1200 feet across, or rather "around," as it has
the shape of a horseshoe. Above the falls are some more
rapids & there the river is one mile wide. It forms the
division between the United States & her Majesty's dominion of Canada. On crossing this bridge on to British soil,

we drove along to the Table Rock quite close to the top of the Horseshoe fall. Here I ascended a tower from which is obtained the finest view of the Horseshoe. Drenching spray, bright with sunshine soon wetted me pretty thoroughly, but who objects to a wetting from Niagara? The rush of water is greater here than in any other part of the falls, owing doubtless to the curved nature of its shape, & very awful is the deep roar from the centre of the curve, where water strikes water as it were in its descent. A man took me into a dressing room & equipped me in a waterproof from head to foot & then escorted me down a long dark shaft with steps in it, & at the bottom, we found ourselves at the foot of the falls & went along a ledge of rock until we were right between the rock & the falling water, but the morning being rather a sharp frost, it was too cold to remain long in this extraordinary position—only worth going into for the sake of saying afterwards, one did it. Yet the grandeur of the immense body of water & the deafening roar were very sublime. Ascended the shaft & stood on the extremity of Table rock, but about 40 feet that used to project over the fall has recently descended into the flood. Recrossed the bridge & had to undergo a verbal examination from the Custom House Officers on my return from British soil to the United States. Then descended a curious incline in a car, to the foot of the American fall, but here the wind was so high & one minute in the spray would wet one to the skin, so I did not stay long, except in a little look-out tower, whence the view was splendid. Ascended this incline & went on to Goat Island, which is reached by a suspension bridge. From this Island some sublime views are obtained of both Falls, but one rock commands the finest sight of the American falls, including the brilliant & perfect rain-bow of which so much has been written, but no power of description can ever pourtray Niagara. As to being dis-

appointed in it, I could almost as much imagine a saint
disappointed in Heaven, as a lover of nature & of nature's
God being other than "First dazzled, then enraptured, then
o'erwhelmed" by this glorious work of Jehovah. I felt all
the while really glad to be alone (as I could not have my
dear wife with me) of course I felt too earnest to talk
& constantly inclined to uncover my head & adoringly ex-
claim, "Great & marvellous are Thy works Lord God
Almighty"! To stand in full view of this wonderful work
of nature & at the same time grasping in its fulness the
wonderful work of His free grace in Jesus & the glorious
salvation through Him, seemed to lift my soul into the
presence chamber of "the King of Kings." From Goat Island
I crossed some small bridges on to the "Three sisters,"
which are little islets commanding no view of the Falls
but right out among the roar & dash of the Rapids above
the Falls, which are full of grandeur & wildness. These
are a mile wide. Various wrecked timber rafts & boats are
caught by the rocks & lie there in testimony of man's
imprudence in trying to get too near the Falls, till caught
in the Rapids. Thence drove back to the Railway suspension bridge, two miles below the Falls & descended a shaft
there to see the Whirlpool Rapids which are very grand.
Paid my Hotel bill, had dinner, & took leave of this marvellous scene with regret. It must be seen to be understood.
One has no idea I think, of the volume of water which
passes over this rocky height. It is estimated that the
depth of water at the Horseshoe fall is 70 feet—I mean
where it rolls over at the top. Thus Lake Erie flows into
Lake Ontario. Took the cars direct from the suspension
bridge for Philadelphia, where I hope to arrive tomorrow
morning. I have written this poor feeble description while
waiting at stations & often when the train was slowly
moving onwards, hence the unusually bad writing, but

the conductor has furnished [me] with a table & lamp which are a great help.

5th day 11th mo 15th The conductor made up our beds at 10 last night & I slept pretty well till nearly 6.30 this morning, when we were approaching our destination. At 8 we reached Philadelphia where John B. Garrett met me & took me to his house where I am to abide probably till 2nd day.[5] His wife is a sweet delicate looking young woman whose Mother lives with them. She is our dear friend Mary Haines.[6] I was pleased to renew my acquaintance with her. After Breakfast, she offered a sweet prayer for me. She is sister to Dr. James Rhoads. J. B. Garrett took me to the depot, whence we went by Rail 10 miles to Haverford. The weekday meeting begins at 11, but we did not arrive till 11.30. but went at once into the gallery, & I soon rose & spoke at length to the interesting company before me, almost all of them students of Haverford College. I think there are 80 or 90 young men now at College. They paid me great & earnest attention. Some of them I knew the parents of, as for instance, sons of Dr. Thomas & James Carey. After closing the meeting in prayer, I went to the college to dinner. Professor Thomas Chase is principal, a wonderfully learned man, one of the American Committee for revising the Scriptures.[7] He is brother to Pliney Chase who I met at Western Y. Meeting. He took us all over the various parts of the College. A

[5] John B. Garrett (1836–1924) was a Philadelphian, educated at Haverford, and married to Hannah Rhoads Haines. A recorded minister, he was deeply concerned about Indians and the Freedmen. He was a bank president and vice president of a railroad. H-DQB.

[6] Mary (Rhoads) Haines (1819–1905) was the widow of William Ellis Haines, who died in 1846. She was principal of the Friends Select School for Girls, and in 1874 accompanied Deborah Thomas (q.v.) on a religious visit to the British Isles. The Friend (Phila.) 79 (1905): p. 40.

[7] Thomas Chase (1827–1892) was born in Massachusetts and educated at Harvard. He was president of Haverford from 1874 to 1886, and a brother of Pliny Earle Chase (q.v.) DAB. H-DQB.

large new building has been just completed, costing 70000 dollars.[8] A tower at its summit commands a beautiful view of the Delaware river & Philadelphia. Returned to the city in the afternoon. The day has been really hot, a wondrous change after the cold of Niagara, but this is called the Indian Summer. Went to tea at R. P. Smith's & H. S. took me to a large Temperance meeting in the evening. While at the Smith's, Dr. Barnabas Hobbs came in. He stays next door at the Whitalls. He is all ready to sail with me next week. I may post one more journal just before sailing. My friends must not be one bit anxious, if we are 14 or even 20 days on the voyage, for the vessels due last 1st day, only arrived here last night, making a 15 & nearly 16 days voyage. I know my dear ones will be praying "Oh! hear us when we cry to Thee, For those in peril on the sea."

6th day 11th mo. 16th Much disappointed at not receiving any home letter yet—the Mail due 5 days ago, but heavy storms at sea are doubtless the cause & our good ship Pensylvania due last 1st day, only arrived here last night 15 days at sea & a gale lasting 8 days, carrying away her davits & some of her boats. But she lay for 16 hours by a wreck to try & render aid & at last had to leave her. The passengers have presented captain Harris with a good chronometer & chain as a thank offering for his efficiency. After reading I called to see the Smiths, also one of my fellow voyagers from England. Then called on Mary Whitall, the dear aged mother of H. S., M. Thomas &c.[9] Her husband John Whitall died this Spring. Hannah Smith took me a lovely drive in her Mother's carriage to Fairmount Park. I dined at Samuel Bettles.[10] He is feeble &

---

[8] Barclay, a new residence hall for students, designed by Addison Hutton, was opened in 1876.

[9] Mary Whitall (1804?–1880). *Friends Review* **33** (1880): p. 457.

[10] Samuel Bettle (1810–1880) a minister belonging to the Twelfth Street Meeting; he had been active in concerns for Indians and Freedmen. H-DQB.

did not join us till after dinner, when he & I had a long
& deeply interesting conversation. He came to see our late
dear Aunt P. G. 17 years ago, I think it was. Back to
John B. Garrett's to tea, James Whitall joining us there.
I called in the evening on Mr & Mrs Kaseby a young
couple who went to England for their wedding tour with
Stanley Pumphrey this Spring & returned to America with
me. They are two earnest Christians with whom I had
much blessed fellowship on board. Then I staid conversing
with Mary Haines till near midnight.

7th day 11th mo: 17th After breakfast, I had a long
call from Marmaduke Cope, who was very cordial &
loving. He came to arrange as to my movements in this
most peculiar meeting, where caution is carried to an
extreme. I consulted him as to a youth's meeting. He
would like it, but dare not have it appointed without
asking all the Elders & of course that would negative it,
as it did when John Hodgkin & P. G. & M. N. made similar
requests & were refused.[11] Called on another fellow passenger Mr Patten, who with his bride had the next cabin
to mine. Then down to the shipping office to know about
sailing &c. Mary Haines took me to a Museum containing
splendid collections of minerals, birds &c. Dined at my
quarters. Then George Vaux called with his daughter
Mary in his carriage & took me a beautiful drive in Fairmount Park, along the shore of the Schuylkill River.[12]
Took my baggage to R. P. Smith's where I am to make
my home till I sail. Young Fowler (a son of H. & Ann
F. Fowler) came to tea with us.[13] In the evening a "parlour

---

[11] John Hodgkin (1800–1875) had been in Philadelphia in 1861. Priscilla
Green, in company with Mary Nicholson (1797–1867) visited the Quaker city
in 1856. L-DQB.

[12] George Vaux (1832–1915) retired from business in order to give his time
to Quaker concerns. He was head of the Bible Association of Friends, was
active in working for the Cheyney Training School, and wrote a number of
historical essays. The *Friend* (Phila.) **88** (1915): p. 524.

[13] Henry and Ann Ford (Barclay) Fowler (1823–1880, 1822–1913). Ann Ford

meeting" of some 50 Friends was held at R. P. Smith's. I was greatly exercised about it, because it was convened to hear *me* teach Scripture truth, & there were present, not only R. P. & H. W. Smith, themselves mighty teachers, but Prof. Pliney Chase, one of the best classical scholars in America & other deeply intellectual Friends. However, He who has never failed me, came to my rescue & we had a blessed meeting. I read 6th Romans, prayed & then expounded. Many Friends asked questions & great freedom was used. H. W. S. closed in prayer, & then followed all sorts of grateful expressions as to the privilege we had enjoyed together. The Smiths & I sat up discussing doctrines & ice-creams till near midnight.

1st day 11th mo: 18th I omitted to mention that on 6th day, I visited an excellent day school, under the care of Friends, called the "Penn Charter School," instituted by the revered "Proprietor & Governor of Pensylvania, William Penn." [14] This morning rose with the feeling that I had 3 meetings to attend to day in Philadelphia, & I felt it indeed a heavy burden, & now, to night, I record how graciously God has dealt with me this day. Robert Smith was very earnest in prayer for a marvellous blessing to accompany me when we knelt in family prayer after breakfast. Went to 12th Street meeting at 10.30 where nearly 600 Friends & others assembled. I was put in the middle of the gallery. After I had prayed, I spoke at great length, & the Friends were very tender & received my message in love. A dear Friend from New England, who I had wanted for years to see, added a few loving words of unity—Rachel Howland, probably *personally* the most beautiful minister in the Society of Friends. Her late mother in law (Susan

---

Fowler was a minister and frequently contributed to the *Friend*. L-DQB, H-DQB.

[14] The William Penn Charter School was located at Twelfth and Market Streets at that time, next to the meetinghouse.

Howland) did not exaggerate on that subject.[15] So the
meeting closed & then came a deluge of loving greetings
from old & young, straight looking elders &c, all clustering
round with words of gratitude for my visit, good old
Edward Bonsall among the rest & Marmaduke Cope, &
the Skulls. I dined at Mary Whitall's, next door to the
Smith's. Her daughter & son-in-law William & Sarah
Nicholson & their family live with her. Then John B.
Garrett called & we walked together to the North Meeting,
one of the largest & straightest in Philadelphia. Samuel
Balderston took me to sit next to him in the gallery & I
never looked on such a sight of long bonnets of the oldest
cut & broad hats all on the heads, & my heart felt ready
to sink, but when I knelt in prayer, I was surprised at the
whole great meeting rising with out an exception. They
often do not, but sit with their hats on, if it is a minister
from the Western Y. Meetings. I then spoke for about an
hour, & I felt as if there was but little opposition, but I
knew my beard & coat would stumble them. A dear little
woman, Rebecca Stokes closed the meeting in praise &
prayer. She took me to tea at her home. She is wife of
John Stokes, a minister & publisher of the "Square
Friend." [16] He could tell me of my Grandmother's texts
& seemed quite kind but is one of the narrowest. Went
to "12th Street" again in the evening & had all the vocal
service in prayer & preaching. Dr. Hobbs sat by my side,
but had nothing to say. Several of my fellow passengers

[15] Rachel Howland (1816?–1902) was born in Burlington, New Jersey, and
moved to New Bedford, Mass., when she married Mathew Howland (1814?–
1884). She was a descendant of James Logan and a recorded minister for
fifty-five years. Susan Howland (1792–1872) traveled in the ministry in Europe
in 1849 and 1857. *American Friend* **9** (1902): p. 696; *Friends Review* **38**
(1884): p. 218. H-DQB.

[16] John S. Stokes (1808?–1892) and Rebecca J. Stokes (1821?–1890) were
stalwart members of this conservative meeting. *The Friend* (Phila.) was called
the "Square Friend" to differentiate it from the one in London. The Friends
at Twelfth Street supported the *Friends Review*. *The Friend* (Phila.) **63** (1890):
p. 232; **65** (1892): p. 376. H-DQB.

at both meetings at "12th Street." I am actually to give my South sea lecture at 12th St. tomorrow evening. At the close of the evening meeting, a dear friend asked me to come & labour in Philadelphia only,—for 3 months!!! Well, God has been indeed good to me, & helped me on this my last sabbath that probably I shall ever spend in America.

2nd day 11th mo: 19th The Howlands are also guests at this sweet home for a day or two & after reading this morning R. P. Smith drove me by his side & inside the carriage his wife & the Howlands to the centennial exhibition building where there is a permanent show of various industries, among others, a beautiful manufacture of glass tumblers, the whole operation of which we watched with great interest.[17] Then drove through Fairmount Park several miles along the Schuylkill river & up a beautiful ravine along a branch of that river called the Wissihicken. This brought us near German Town where my kind friends left me at Dr. Rhoads & took back my Portmanteau with Winter clothes for the voyage, which I had left there, when I first landed. It was nice to have an hour or two with the good Dr. & his wife. I dined at Marmaduke Cope's. His son-in-law Anthony & A.K.'s son Duke, dined with us, also J. Whitall's wife. Called on A.K.'s invalid wife for awhile. She keeps her bedroom & then on the aged father of Robert P. Smith. Back by Rail to Philadelphia. Joined at tea by George & Lizzie Tatum of Woodbury. She is Joseph & Isabella Jones's eldest daughter, the only one of his family I had not seen before coming here. In the evening went to 12th Street meeting, where to an audience of (I suppose) fully 500 Friends & others, I gave a missionary lecture, which was most warmly received. Staid talking to my dear host & hostess till near midnight & closed with fervent prayer from R. P. Smith.

---

[17] The Centennial Exhibition to commemorate the signing of the Declaration of Independence in 1776.

3rd day 11th mo 20th I omitted to mention, that in
walking along Arch Street one day I looked over a fence
into an old graveyard & read these words on a perfectly
plain flat stone: "Benjamin & Deborah Franklin 1790."
This is all that marks the resting place of that great man.
This morning I went to breakfast at Elizabeth Sharpless's
where were Ann Taylor & Mary Bettle to meet me, &
we had a very satisfactory time. Then I went to the ferry
& crossed the Delaware in a ferry steamer to New Jersey
state where I took the train, 20 miles to the little old
fashioned town of Burlington. There I found a carriage
& pair waiting for me & I was soon driven out two miles
to the beautiful home of a very much revered Friend &
was ushered into the noble presence of Eliza P. Gurney.
She gave me a very loving welcome & I was truly glad to
visit her. She has two nieces of her own living with her,
one a miss Kirkbride & the other a young widow, whose
husband only lived about a year after they married &
has left her with a sweet, but sickly little girl. Rebecca
Collins was staying there. Eliza Gurney looks wonderfully
well for 78. A flush of healthy colour still ornaments her
placid face. I sat & talked with her of home interests &
then religiously, for nearly 3 hours, when we went in to
dinner. Then she gave me a beautiful photo. of herself,
& a copy of Whittier's Poems, & sent me to Burlington in
her carriage, again. Reached Philadelphia at 4.30 & did
some packing up, then to tea at Joshua Bailey's.[18] He
is one of the few Friends in this city, who ventures to mark
out a course for himself & having great wealth he con-
secrates to his Lord, feeds 4000 poor people every day;
has a large temperance & mission room which he manages
himself, entirely. After tea, he took me to his mission room
where we held a meeting, largely attended—many Friends

---

[18] Joshua L. Baily (1826–1916) was in the dry goods business, and gave
himself to many concerns. He was president of the American Bible Society.
H-DQB.

there, even some from North Meeting. I preached for about an hour to a very solemn & attentive audience. We had Bible reading & hymns. John Garrett closed in prayer. I was surprised & pleased to see Dr. Watson come in. He said he had seen my name in the Paper & wished to hear me again. He was the Episcopal divine on board the Pensylvania from England. Another sweet communion with R.P. & H.W. Smith before retiring. It is indeed a heavenly privilege to make one's home with them.

4th day 11th mo. 21st Went to breakfast at David Sculls. His son Edward we knew in England as companion to Rufus King.[19] Then to call on next door neighbours the Simpsons who were of my fellow passengers from home. Found a letter from my dear wife on my return—the last I hope, till I reach the other side of the Atlantic. At 10.30 went to 12th St. Monthly Meeting which was attended by about 600 Friends (wishing to see me I am told) three times its ordinary size. Barnabas Hobbs offered prayer & then I spoke a long while. B.H. added a little & John Garrett prayed very beautifully for abundant fruit in this land to my labours & for safe voyaging for us both. So closed the last public assembly of worshippers, I expect ever to be present at, in this land. At the Discipline meeting I presented my certificates which were read & sent into the Women's meeting. Many Friends expressed their unity with me & thankfulness for my visit & a Minute was made of my "acceptable company & Gospel labours, &c." It was an interesting Mo. Meeting—a Committee appointed to visit families &c. After a touching number of farewells from dear friends I went to the shipping office & find the Pensylvania sails at 9.A.M. tomorrow. B.H. & I, each have a cabin to ourselves, as there are only 20 passengers. I dined at Edward Bonsall's. He is 83 years old, a widower & lives with his sister Potts & her family. Her daughter

---

[19] David Scull (1799–1884). *Friends Review* **38** (1885): p. 601.

Anna was a special friend of our late dear Aunt P. Green.[20]
Thence to my quarters to pack up & get ready for posting
letters which may reach home a day or two before I do.
I am leaving America with a very thankful heart, in good
bodily health, enjoying the hard frost which night & day
prevails here, now, the weather cloudless. Of my last few
hours I must tell when permitted to reach home, as a party
of Friends are asked to spend the evening with me, &
dear Mary Thomas of Baltimore has just arrived.

[20] Edward Bonsall (1795–1879). *Friends Review* **32** (1879): p. 681.

IX. Homeward Voyage

4th day 11th Mo: 21st After dispatching my last home budget a party of Friends arrived at R. P. Smiths to spend my last evening with me in earnest religious converse & prayer. Dr. Rhoads & his sister Mary Haines, Matthew & Rachel Howland, Eli Johnson (who is Rhoda Coffins brother and Mary Johnson's husband) Joshua Bailey & wife, James Whitall, W. & S. Nicholson, John B. Garrett & my dear friend from Baltimore, Mary W. Thomas were among the number.[1] We had much very profitable & holy communion, & several prayers, especially for a safe voyage & joyful home welcome for me & prayer for my future usefulness &c. Then a very touching leave taking & I retired to finish packing up which, with various gifts from dear friends &c. is no light job.

5th day 22nd Mary Thomas & John B. Garrett joined us at breakfast, after which we had a blessed season of prayer & praise. Then I took leave of Hannah W. Smith who has gone to day, to hold a series of meetings at Brooklyn. B. Hobbs, Robert P. Smith & I went in Mary Whitall's carriage to the wharf where were many Friends gathered to take a last look at us. I had a very hearty welcome on board the good old Pensylvania, from officers & Captain & when I went below felt as much at home as if the three months since I left the ship was all a dream. At 9 A.M. all who were not passengers were ordered on shore & we began at once slowly to move away. When outside the wharf our cannon fired & with waving handkerchiefs & cheers, we

---

[1] Mary (Coffin) Johnson (b. 1834) married Eli Johnson (1830–1901) in 1852. Mary was the sister of Charles F. Coffin, and Eli the brother of his wife, Rhoda Johnson Coffin (*q.v.*), *Reminiscences*, p. 11. James Whitall (1834–1896) was a glass manufacturer and active in many Quaker concerns. *Biog. Cat. Haverford.* William H. Nicholson (1827–1908) married Sarah Whitall (1833–1886) in 1855. *Biog. Cat. Haverford.*

steamed away from Philadelphia. The Delaware River &
Bay are not beautiful, New Jersey & Delaware States being
very flat and marshy, like Cambridgeshire. At 6 P.M. we had
sent our pilot on shore at Cape Henlopen & by bedtime
had lost sight of Cape May Lighthouse & with it, of the
American continent.

6th day 23rd Out of 22 passengers, there were only 4
at breakfast—all the others very sick. The wind from the
time we left the Delaware, being in our teeth & blowing
almost a gale. But the weather is clear & sunny & not a
very heavy sea on. Barnabas Hobbs was the first to be
sick last evening & is very prostrate to day. We are each
blessed with a separate Stateroom which is a great luxury.

7th day 24th The wind still dead on end retards our
homeward progress & besides, increases the ship's motion,
so that we have very little company on deck, & what we
have is somewhat sickly & uncomfortable. Dr. Hobbs I
have persuaded to lie to day in the companion way (alias
"Social Hall") & as he eats a little, I presume he is better.
I have had a good deal of converse with him, as he seems
able to bear it.

1st day 25th A high wind right in our teeth, rendering
almost everyone sea-sick & no probability of any religious
service. I spent the day quietly, sometimes conversing
seriously with the few passengers able to be on deck or
in the smoking room. One old gentleman, Mr. Verga from
Delaware, is a Roman Catholic, but very open to religious
converse. He lent me his prayerbook & I told him my views
as to the blessed Virgin & saints &c. Dr. Hobbs in bed &
all the ladies to day. The Captain asked me about a service.
Of course I told him I would like it if possible, but as night
came on, it was out of the question.

2nd day 26th A bright sunny morning but bitterly cold.
Saw 14 whales spouting a little distance from the ship.

Got my friend Dr. Hobbs into the Social Hall for a little while.

27th & 28th Little to report of interest. We are making a slow voyage & it seems unlikely we can get to Liverpool till the middle of next week. This is a disappointment to me, as I know my dearest ones will be anxiously waiting my coming, but head winds & big seas sadly hinder our progress, while the gulf stream is against us instead of being in our favour. We have I think only 19 1st class passengers. Dr. Barnabas Hobbs, Justus Strawbridge a Friend of Philadelphia (Germanstown) going over to England on business,[2] Mr. Morphy, the Spanish Consul with his lady & 4 very little children, Mr. Lewis, an Englishman, Mr. Verga, Miss Bull, Mrs. Burtt & her three daughters, two of them young women, Mr. & Mrs. Kaufmann & a young lad of 17 called "Charlie" & W. Robson. But I do not blame people for not crossing in the Winter, if they can avoid it. The weather is so cold & rough & the nights so long & dark. Yesterday & to day we have managed some games of "Shuffle board" on deck, for exercise. The brilliant sun which rose this morning without a cloud, is now hidden behind a very vapoury looking atmosphere, reminding one of an English November.

5th day 29th After dinner this evening our Captain suddenly asked me to give a lecture on the South Sea Islands, in the Saloon. Of course I consented & the passengers expressed themselves much pleased. We have one or two gentlemen on board who are sadly too fond of beer & are drinking all day. I have spoken very freely to three of them & I am thankful to say, they have taken it very

[2] Justus C. Strawbridge (1838–1911) started his business career working for Joshua L. Baily (q.v.). He opened his own business in 1862 and joined with Isaac H. Clothier (1837–1921) in 1868 to found the department store Strawbridge and Clothier. The fact that one was a member of the Orthodox Yearly Meeting and the other Race Street Yearly Meeting made this partnership unusual. *American Friend* **18** (1911): p. 213. H-DQB.

kindly & I hope may profit. At any rate, they are drinking much less since I spoke.

6th day 11th mo: 30th Came on deck this morning to find the weather warm as Summer, really warmer than on the voyage out in August; and a perfect calm & nearly cloudless. As the day went on however, it began to blow & at night we had a heavy gale from the West, but as we rushed along with it, all sails set, did not feel much of it except the tremendous rolling. Made a splendid run to day.

12 th mo: 1st Took Dr. Hobbs over the ship & to inspect our great engines after breakfast. He is a man who takes great interest in all that pertains to a ship & its working. The last two or three days we have had a great deal of singing & music, our Consul's lady being a splendid pianist, but hymns seem rather new to her, while Verdi's La Traviata & Il Trovatore she has at her fingers ends. But Sankey's hymns are constantly being sung by some of us & especially during the long dark evenings when the Captain is singing with us.

1st day 12th mo: 2nd At 10.45 the gong sounded for Divine service in the Saloon, & several intermediate & steerage passengers & all our first cabin companions but one, were present. The Captain read prayers & I read the two lessons for the day. After "Rock of Ages" & "Nearer my God to thee" had been sung, I preached for nearly half an hour & Barnabas Hobbs offered a most beautiful prayer for all on board, the Captain, Officers & men, & all passengers. So closed the service, at which were present *most* Episcopalians, some Quakers Jews & Romanists. It was a good time. To night, we are expecting to sight Fastnet Lighthouse on a rock off the Irish coast & to reach Queenstown early tomorrow morning. If not detained there, shall, by the good providence of God, reach Liverpool at midnight tomorrow & lodge on board, so as to take an early train to London on 3rd day. It is calm & quiet

to day, no sea on & almost no wind. The voyage a day
longer than usual owing to the contrary winds the first few
days, but wonderfully calm & warm for almost midwinter.

2nd day 12th Mo: 3rd At 10 last night we saw the
brilliant light of Cape Fastnet lighthouse & soon sent up
a rocket & fired off three Roman candles, the signal of
our ship's company & after a short pause, saw a rocket
in reply sent up from the coast. Our captain says we are
reported already, both in London & Philadelphia. At 3 o'clk
this morning we reached Queenstown & I sent off letters
& a telegram to tell my dear ones of our safe arrival on this
side of the Atlantic. Through some mistake, the wrong
letters were sent us from Queenstown directed to the
passengers on some other ship, while those to us were
doubtless sent to them instead. Went to bed again & on
coming on deck before breakfast, saw the long line of
Irish coast, looking very bright & sunny, while a background of fine bold mountains made our approach to my
dear native home very attractive. Games of shuffle board
&c. on deck occupied most of the day & as evening came on
& we lost sight of Ireland & came in full view of the Welch
coast & Snowdonia we felt getting very near home. The
evening was dark; thick & foggy so that Holyhead light
looked almost like a comet as it slowly shone out & then
vanished & anon appeared again. As I was pacing our
deck alone about 7 P.M., thinking of past & future, America,
our voyage & my bright welcome home so nearly at hand,
I noticed the one sharp ring of the gong in the Engine
room which means "Stop her" & directly after the double
ring for "full steam astern," instantly our fog horn sounded,
& then there was an awful crash, so violent, that some of
our passengers were thrown down. I knew we had had a
collision & ran to the side to see whether the water was
rising & we were going down, but on looking ahead,
discovered the white sails & tall masts of a large sailing

vessel, one mast fallen over, while our vessel had cut her half in two, about midships. It was an awful sight, & every moment seemed like an hour almost. As we backed through the water, the ship stuck to us enabling her captain to clamber up into our bows & assist his wife & son up after him, while several of their sailors followed. I think nine in all, were rescued in that manner. No sooner had our vessel backed itself loose from the ship, than we saw her settle rapidly down—down down, till the light on her foremast was extinguished beneath the waves. I suppose the Pensylvania had not struck the Oasis more than five minutes before the latter had sunk in the dark, deep waters. Then came the awful reflection that the poor men whose cries we had just heard for "help" & "send us your boats" were left to battle with the ocean, or to die. I never experienced anything so terrible, the intense darkness, the utter helplessness of us, passengers, to assist & the thought of souls (perhaps) unprepared that might be soon passing away & the dear ones they might have just left, seemed more than one could bear, yet a sense of the Lord's keeping Power never left me, for which I now record my heartfelt thankfulness. I went into B. C. Hobbs's cabin & said to him "it is a blessed thing at such a time as this" he at once said, "to feel God's Keeping Power, it is indeed." Some of our fellow passengers were sadly upset. Mr. Lewis had been drinking & clung to me foolishly, so that I had to tell him not to be silly but to go & lie down, if he could not behave. Our Captain's cry, "down with the boats, boys. It is life or death" was heartily responded to, so that in six minutes, five of our boats were in the water, well manned & a bright lantern in each. Then began an hour of intense anxiety as we watched the lights glimmer over the dark waters & at length we saw a horrid looking black object so close to us, that we steamed forward a few fathoms & then found it was the stern of the "Oasis," stand-

ing up out of the sea. As she was only in ballast, laden
with sand & stones, we suppose, as she went down head
first, she shot out her cargo, & thus her stern rose when
empty. After a tedious wait, one boat returned, with the
dismal cry, "We cant find any one Sir." Then came a second
with the same report. The third had picked up several,
& so had the fourth. Then came the fifth with two poor
fellows & a cat. One man quite black & senseless with
exposure, having been floating on a ladder for a long while.
Our boat would have passed him by but hearing a cat mew,
thought they would save the poor creature (sailors have a
great veneration for cats.) They rowed up to where she
was mewing & found her sitting on a poor man's head,
he unconscious & of course unable to make any noise. So
the cat saved his life by God's good providence, & now,
on asking the Captain of the Oasis, he said they had 18
souls on board & had found a stowaway since sailing from
Liverpool that morning, & we had the unspeakable comfort
of knowing that they were all saved & safe on board our
steamship & our Dr. busy restoring to life the poor half
drowned men. The *bitterness* of the trouble was then
over, but we were all much unnerved & when tea was
announced at 9. instead of 7. we had no sort of relish for
it. A stunned feeling, a kind of horror was on us all. The
Captain of the Oasis was very poorly & was resting when
we struck his ship. He seized his wife & got into our bows,
not waiting to put on hat or boots, & she, poor thing, was
very thinly clad & with nothing on her head. She nearly
fainted when they first led her aft into the Social Hall. She
was sadly regretting her gold watch, her purse & (as she
said) all her valuables gone to the bottom of the sea. Our
Captain gave them a spare state room & every possible
comfort; while a voluntary levy was paid by us male
passengers, of any old clothing for the poor half drowned
sailors. After a delay of some two hours, sufficient to make

it impossible to get over the bar with the evening tide, we steamed very slowly forward, blowing our fog horn dismally every two or three minutes & often stopping & reversing steam. An undefined sense of peril made us long for the day, a feeling of how possible some other vessel might cut us in two as we had done the Oasis, & the almost certainty that many of us would never see land in that case, till the fiat go forth to the sea to give up its dead! Most of us sat talking & trying to be cheerful in the saloon till nearly 3 o'clk on 3rd morning 12th mo: 4th when we dropped anchor just outside the bar, at Liverpool, the Captain had kindly allowed our saloon & cabin lights to be left burning, for somehow it seemed not nice to be in the dark.

Rose at 7 o'clk & found our anchor just up & we commenced steaming slowly up the Mersey through a dense fog, sounding, & blowing the horn every minute. Breakfast about 7 o'clk & by 8. we were alongside of two steam tugs, one to take the steerage & one the 1st class passengers to shore. A short & hurried leave taking of Captain & officers & we left our good ship & were soon alongside the great landing stage.

Our English custom house officers are not so particular as those at Philadelphia, so that B. Hobbs & I were scarce five minutes before we & our luggage were deposited in a cab & driving along the streets of Liverpool. Stopped at the Shipping office to tell of our accident & to assure the managers that Captain Harris was in no way to blame. Then on to the L. & N.W. Station & thence by Express to London. B.C. Hobbs & I having much religious converse & much interesting interchange of sentiment on this, his first introduction to dear old England.

J.B. Braithwaite met us at Euston Square & here I parted from Dr. Hobbs, leaving him with J.B.B. I took a cab to Liverpool St. & there in the waitingroom had the unspeakable pleasure of meeting my precious wife, who in answer to a telegram I had sent her from Liverpool, had come up to welcome & escort me home.

Dined together, & reached Audley End at about 8 P.M. thence to our dear home in the Brougham. God has been very gracious to my dearest ones while I have been away. My beloved Parents & Priscie were at home to meet me & they & my five little darlings (who I kissed in their own little beds to night) are all in usual health.

And now, what can I render to the Lord for all His care of me by sea & land during the 12000 miles I have travelled in the last four months? He has greatly favored me as a Minister & made my service for Him generally acceptable, & then He has blessed my own soul with a wondrous realization of the exceeding greatness of His power even to me, baptizing me with the Holy Ghost & teaching me in a way I never experienced before—the completeness & fulness of the salvation wrought for us & in us, by His dear Son Jesus Christ. May His felt presence ever keep me, His poor child, watchful, humble, prayerful, abiding in Him & He in my heart by faith, that so I may reflect His image, myself nothing—Himself ALL. & my precious Saviour be abundantly glorified, who with our loving Father in Heaven & the Holy Spirit is forever worthy.

INDEX

The abbreviation "Y.M." for Yearly Meeting has been made throughout. There are no special references to footnotes.